COVENANT & CALL

MISSION OF THE FUTURE CHURCH

MARY ELIZABETH MULLINO MOORE

WITH

EUN HYE CHOI, GRANT HAGIYA, CORNISH ROGERS,

LILY VILLAMIN, AND LYDIA WATERS

DISCIPLESHIP RESOURCES

P.O. BOX 340003 • NASHVILLE, TN 37203-0003
www.discipleshipresources.org

Cover design by Sharon Anderson

Book design by Nanci Lamar

Edited by Linda R. Whited and Cindy S. Harris

ISBN 0-88177-272-0

Library of Congress Catalog Card No. 98-88818

Scripture quotations, unless otherwise indicated, are from the New Revised Standard Version of the Bible, copyright © 1989 by the Division of Christian Education of the National Council of the Churches of Christ in the USA. All rights reserved. Used by permission.

DR272

CONTENTS

PREFACE

For several years I have been working on a major study of the church. In the midst of that research, the opportunity came to write this book. I wanted to invite people to wrestle with visions and possibilities for the church's life; this was my chance. I was challenged by the image of a wide range of readers wrestling together with what it means to be church. I hoped that the readers would be laity, leaders, questioners, and clergy of the church. My hope was that the book would make a difference, not by itself but through the reflections it would evoke. My hope was that the book, and people's interactions with it, would be rooted in God's Spirit and in covenant community. My hope was that the book could contribute to the church's self-understanding and could encourage the church to be faithful to God's calling—to minister in a hurting world and to contribute to a more just and loving future.

Little did I know that the research and writing of this book would be so evocative for me. I spent several months writing the first draft, and then I began to work with the consulting team. I knew they would be insightful, but I was overwhelmed by their power of observation and their significant contributions. One of the team said to me, "This is a very white book, even though you have drawn admirably from different cultures and parts of the world." I asked, "Is it a hopelessly white book?" She replied, "No, I think we can help you!"

That one story reveals the heart of this book—living in covenant community. When Lydia Waters said those words to me, she was not trying to insult or belittle me; she was doing exactly what I had asked of her. She was trying to help me see a larger picture—a communal picture. To that reminder was added Lily Villamin's descriptions of how Filipino society functions. Then, to keep me grounded, Cornish Rogers urged for more concreteness and clarity of definitions, and Eun Hye Choi advocated to keep the theological language closely connected to the church's life. At the same time, Grant Hagiya raised the issue of how one book can address and challenge a broad audience of laity, clergy, theological questioners, and people who prefer a more straightforward discourse. The team members did not always agree with one another, but the basic directions of their suggestions were united—to reflect the fullness and diversity of community, and to do so with concreteness and theological substance. Their contributions are woven into the entire fabric of the book. The result is a deeper and more focused work; I am grateful beyond measure.

In addition, I am grateful to Henk Pieterse, Linda Whited, and Cindy Harris, who made invaluable editorial suggestions as I wrote, and to Sungyi Choi, who made helpful suggestions on the Invitation and provided bibliographic assistance on the entire manuscript. Leah Fowler was a lifesaver in helping with permission requests and the final editing process. Many churches and church leaders have also contributed to this book. Some of them are named in the book, and others have contributed by inspiration, encouragement, and question-posing. To these thanks, I add inexpressible gratitude for my family, who persevered during a year when I was writing and we were preparing to move across country. Most of our summer vacation and a part of box-packing time were given to the completion of this manuscript. Allen and Rebecca especially made space in their lives so that I could make space in mine. Allen also commented helpfully on the entire manuscript. The two of them experienced some of the trials of covenant living, and their mark is clearly on this book.

These words of thanksgiving reveal something about the book's theme; one person could not possibly have written it. The book is not only about covenant and call; it is created by and for covenant community. We on the writing team see ourselves as participating in an ancient prophetic tradition: calling people back to covenant. We dedicate this book to the prophets of old and the ordinary prophets around us, who courageously return to covenant and are transformed by the very God who calls them. Our hope now is that the book will be a blessing and prophetic call to you and to the future church!

Mary Elizabeth Mullino Moore
January 6, 2000

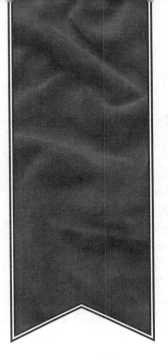

CALLED TO COVENANT

After my father died, Mother was able to return to regular participation in church. When she returned, however, she could not be as active as she had once been. She no longer had the energy to teach Sunday school or give book reviews. She did return with eagerness, however; and during those first months, she contributed largely by receiving. One group welcomed her into their Sunday school class. Several younger folks also reached out to her, a source of great delight. Ushers met her at the door and walked her to the front of the sanctuary. All of these people became friends, and Mother began to experience her local church as a covenant community.

The purpose of this chapter is to introduce the covenantal theme of the book. Covenant community is a gift from God, through which people are bound in relationship and responsibility with God, one another, and all of God's creation. Covenant can exist in small ways, as in my mother's story; it can also be far-reaching, as in God's enduring covenant with Israel and God's covenant of new life in Jesus Christ. All these covenants are important to God. The central affirmation of this book is that *the church, as the body of Christ, is a covenant community called to live faithfully toward God's new creation.*

In the oldest of our Scriptures, we find God making covenant with the people of Israel, not one by one but as a whole people. When God did come to individuals, it was to enter into covenant with the whole people. Abraham and Sarah were called to become father and mother of a great nation; Moses and David were called to lead the Israelites in times of trouble; and Jesus was called to point the people—Jews and Gentiles alike—to the ways of God and God's future. What is covenant, then? As we see in biblical covenants, God comes to people and to all creation, enters communal relationship, calls them to serve God's purposes in the world, and empowers them to move toward God's future. These four qualities of covenant echo throughout this chapter.

The actual forms of covenant have varied from time to time and place to place. We celebrate covenants of baptism, Communion (Eucharist), confirmation, marriage, commissioning, ordination, and more. In all of these, people are bound to God, and they are bound with one another. In light of such rich tradition, this book is intended to encourage people in covenantal living and engage them in discerning and responding to God's call.

One might understand covenant better by looking to communal cultures of our day—cultures where the spirit of covenant is very much alive. In the Philippines, when a family needs to move their stilt house, everyone in the community helps. Some move the house while others provide food and drink. In the Tagalog language, the word that describes this common act is *katipunan*— unity for the sake of a cause, or unity to serve humanity. Another important expression in Tagalog is *pakikisama*, referring to the cooperation that people exercise to honor one another. *Pakikisama* is not an act of obligation but of respect for an honored friend. The

Covenant and Call

recipient of such honor also gives honor to the giver simply by receiving. One finds a similar spirit in Africa, where the Swahili word *harambee* is a watchword across the continent. It means "let us pull together." In Kenya this is the national motto. People call one another to a spirit of *harambee* in order to install a water pump in their village, to cooperate in national affairs, or to act together in the church.

One might further imagine the meaning of covenant through a story from a United Methodist congregation in the Slovak Republic (the eastern portion of the former Czechoslovakia). The pastor of this congregation, Pavel Prochazka, is a Slovak citizen and is Superintendent of United Methodist Churches in his newly reconstituted nation. He serves a congregation in the capital city of Bratislava and visits frequently with others. At the same time, he translates and publishes *The Book of Discipline* in the Slovakian language, visits state schools to offer religious education, speaks in a rotation with other Christian and Jewish leaders on public radio, counsels with the Slovakian Ministry of Culture, and teaches in an ecumenical theological seminary. In many of these activities, such as translating, publishing, and teaching, members of Pavel's congregation join him. In the theological school, theologians and church leaders from other Christian denominations join in the work. All of these people are dedicated to providing theological education in their native language.

This story reveals much about covenant. Pavel and his congregation are people of prayer, people who give thanks to God every day for the simple gift of life. They are also conscious of themselves as part of a long line of God's people stretching back to Abraham and Sarah and to the beginning of creation. They further see themselves as a particular people with challenging opportunities to be faithful in their newly established country. They witness to their faith in worship and conversation. As a people, they live in partnership with one another, with leaders of their Slovak schools and public works, with ecumenical church leaders, and with leaders of other faiths. They do all these things in response to God's gift of life and God's expectations of people to be responsible. They live in covenant—initiated and held together by God, and lived by humans who respond to God and join with one another to contribute to the well-being of the world.

This congregation represents well the four qualities that are normally associated with covenant: God's gracious act through which the covenant relationship is established; a consequent bonding of God with creation; a distinctively faithful and ethical relationship between God and humanity, with mutual expectations; and a vision of God's future of justice, righteousness, and love. One cannot say that the congregation in Bratislava is perfect in its covenantal living, but they are certainly intentional and faithful. As such, they are able to inspire others and point to the possibility of covenant incarnated in ordinary congregations. With those covenantal images in mind, we turn now to explore covenant in relation to God, and then to the calling of Christian people.

Covenant and the God of Relationships

Covenant is born in a God who is relational through and through. This relational God creates the world; feels the groans of creation; loves, liberates, and sustains a broken world; and comes to us as One and More than One—Trinity. Although the concept of Trinity was a construct of the early Christian church, the concept of many names and dimensions in the life of God runs deep in Jewish and Christian traditions. We now turn to some of these dimensions as a way of being alert to the multifaceted nature of God, who is known to Jews, Christians, and Muslims alike as One.

One Who Creates

In addition to the familiar creation stories in Genesis 1:1–2:4a, Genesis 2:4b-25, and Proverbs 8:22-31, the Bible abounds with references to God's work of creation, both in the beginning and throughout time. Consider Psalm 100. Here we find a song of remembrance and a call to praise:

> Know that the LORD is God.
> It is he that made us, and we are his;

we are his people, and the sheep of his pasture.

(Psalm 100:3)

Note that in this one verse, God is identified five times. God is named as Lord, then as Creator. Then the relationship of people to God is emphasized in a three-fold song: we are God's; we are God's people; we are sheep of God's pasture. The poetic refrain moves from the holiness and creativity of God to the relationship of God with the people. The relationship is named three times in three different ways, suggesting fullness and completeness. The poetry points to God's covenant, grounded in God's act of creation and the consequent relationship of people to their maker.

One Who Delights and Laments

In the Bible we receive a vivid image of God as One who responds. In the beginning, God is shown as one who delights in creation, pronouncing the creation good (Genesis 1:4, 10, 12, 18, 21, 25, 31). Later, when the Israelites are slaves in Egypt, God is shown as one who laments with the people. God speaks to Moses from a burning bush:

> I have observed the misery of my people who are in Egypt;
> I have heard their cry on account of their taskmasters.
> Indeed, I know their sufferings, and I have come down to
> deliver them from the Egyptians, and to bring them up out
> of that land to a good and broad land, a land flowing with
> milk and honey.
> (Exodus 3:7-8; see also Exodus 2:23-25; 3:9-10)

Here we see God lamenting the plight of the people. The picture is intimate—not a distant observation. The verbs in verse 7 alone reveal an intimate knowing on the part of God, who observed, heard, and knew. Then in verse 8, we read of a very active response on the part of God, who came down to deliver the people and to bring them up out of that land. The God portrayed in this passage, as in much of the biblical witness, is a God who feels and laments the pain of the people. Further, God responds, and God sends others (as Moses) to respond. The story points to

God's covenant, which is grounded in God's feeling for people who suffer. God is One who delights and laments!

One Who Loves, Liberates, and Sustains

The story of Moses and the burning bush leads directly to God's deliverance of the people from slavery and to God's other active works of loving, liberating, and sustaining the people and creation. These are stories of miracles and ordinary moments—of dramatic rescues from slavery and forty years of wandering in the desert (Exodus 4:1–40:38). These are stories of God's listening to Job's troubles, responding to Job with dramatic reminders that God is God, and then restoring Job's life (Job 31; 38–42). These are stories of a baby, Jesus, born in a stable with the jubilation of angels and wise men and the quiet delight of his parents (Luke 2:1-20; Matthew 1:18–2:12). These are stories of Jesus' teaching and healing, explaining himself again and again to the disciples, who did not understand.

These are also the stories of Pentecost, when the Spirit of God rushed into the house where Jesus' followers gathered, with a rushing sound like a violent wind and with tongues like fire resting upon each person, filling all of them with the Holy Spirit (Acts 2:1-4). These are stories of young Christian churches trying to find their way in their new faith through squabbles, celebrations, and earnest debates. These are stories of people in the same churches who continued to teach, preach, heal, and serve, revealing the continuing work of God among them—loving, liberating, sustaining them still.

One Who Is More Than One—Trinity

The biblical images of God that have been identified thus far are rich in themselves, but the early Christian community evoked an additional image of God as Three-in-One, or Trinity. Much has been written about the Trinity in nearly two thousand years of Christian history, and much mystification has taken place; however, the concept of Trinity is grounded in the earthy human experience of God.

At the very heart of the trinitarian idea is the notion that God is a community. The Orthodox theologian John Zizioulas explains, "The *nature* of God is communion."[1] Because God is a community of three persons, the very being of God reveals what human community is to be: a community that delights in the distinctiveness of each person and the fullness of communion. Within Orthodox Christian communities, this concept becomes the core of all theology; theologies of the church and of family relationships all emerge from trinitarian ground. The trinitarian image inspires human relationships that are distinctly personal and fully communal.

One United Methodist pastor expresses this idea in practical terms when she explains why she is so content serving congregations rather than applying her Ph.D. in a steady stream of academic meetings. She says of her life in the church: "The diversity of people, the diversity of need, the diversity of opinion, and the different valuing of what makes life worth living seem more intense to me now, away from academics."[2] The pastor who penned these words has found something in the community of an ordinary congregation that mirrors the community of Trinity. She would be the first to say that her New York congregations are not ideal communities, nor are academic communities necessarily abstract and sterile. Her point is more earthy, namely that congregations have rich textures within them, mirroring the depths of life and, thus, revealing God.

The God of relationships is more than an interesting idea; the God of relationships challenges us to be who we were created to be and to follow God's ways in all that we do. For this reason, we will reflect more deeply on God as Trinity in Chapter Three as we explore theological convictions that anchor covenantal communities. What is most important here is to recognize the ways in which our images and ideas of God are interwoven with our actions as we live in human communities and seek to be faithful. This connection between theology and human action leads naturally to the theme of covenant and call.

God's Covenant and Call

The center of this book is covenant and call—two realities, inextricably linked. Covenant and call are never abstract; they are always embodied in living stories. To explore the fullness of covenant and call, we begin with two stories and interpret them in relation to biblical and historical traditions.

Consider first the story of a congregation in Los Angeles that was severely affected by the civil uprising in April 1992. The people of Holman United Methodist Church found themselves, in the midst of the uprising, surrounded by smoke and stories of fear and hurt. Many in the church were directly affected; they were also aware of hundreds of hurting people who lived or worked nearby. A predominantly African American congregation, the people of Holman prayed fervently. They knew God's presence and felt compelled to respond. In the first hours, they responded directly to the cries around them. Soon after, the church developed teams of people who were prepared to listen, provide counseling services, and offer guidance for people in need. The church was uniquely able to offer these caring teams because of the immediacy of their own experience, the strength of their concern, and the expertise in the congregation for community leadership.

Less than two years later, the Northridge earthquake shook Southern California. Once again many people were affected by fear and hurt. This time the people who were most affected lived a few miles away from the center of Los Angeles, though the effects traveled throughout the region, as had the effects of the uprising. Holman United Methodist Church rose to the occasion again. They reactivated their caring teams and provided services to people in the areas hardest hit by the earthquake. What had begun as a response to one emergency became a way of living and sharing with others.

The second covenant story is found in the collaborative actions of two churches—one in California and one in South Africa. The California church is Foothills United Methodist Church, a suburban church that is lively in its ministry and growing in spirit and numbers. Several years ago, a group within this largely European-

American church felt a strong call to minister beyond themselves. The nudging seemed to come from God, so they prayed. Eventually, they initiated a month-long journey to Alaska to work alongside churches there. In time, a South African pastor came to the Foothills Church for a short period of interim service. During this time, friendships were born and the South African pastor challenged the Foothills congregation to come help his own white congregation find the joy of outreach mission. Communication between the South African pastor and his friends soon spread throughout the two congregations, and the idea for a work team was born. The white South African congregation—seeking to live into the new South Africa—was happy to host the work team from California and support their work.

All was arranged, and the work team arrived, bringing money they had raised for materials. They were hosted grandly by the white Port Elizabeth congregation, who described the team's work. Then the California team was sent on their way. They worked for two weeks with the people in a nearby South African village, building a parsonage for the village's first full-time pastor (a woman). They made new friends in the village and then invited the Port Elizabeth congregation to join in a celebration on the last day. Although the Port Elizabeth folk had never been involved in such ministries, they joined enthusiastically in sharing joy and food and clothes. The party culminated with "Amazing Grace," raising the roof. Everyone parted, better friends than ever.

A few months passed and communication continued between the South Africa and California congregations. One day an excited letter arrived from the Port Elizabeth pastor, describing the enthusiastic decision of his church to become partners with the people in the village where their California sisters and brothers had been. They were going to spend time during the next month working alongside people in the village, and on a regular basis thereafter. What had begun as a one-time act of mercy was becoming a long-term partnership and a growing friendship across racial and socioeconomic lines.

In both of these stories, themes of covenant and call are revealed. In particular, covenant is revealed as initiated by God, binding communities, calling people to action, and pointing to the future. In both stories, the people saw God in the midst of their action. In both, the people were bound with God and one another, and their sense of community deepened as they acted together. In both stories, the congregations experienced a strong call to action—vigorous and sustained. And in both stories, the churches' work stirred a vision, even inspiring others to engage in similar action.

Initiated by God

In the Holman Church story, the people prayed fervently. They felt compelled to pray; and through prayer, they felt compelled to act. Similarly, the inspiration for the Foothills Church to initiate partnerships with African churches was inspired by a strong sense of God's call, experienced first by a small group within the congregation. Both of these churches were conscious of a reality that is frequently named in the Bible: *God takes initiative in covenantal relationships.* Three major dimensions of this reality are considered here, drawing from the biblical and historical witness.

First, *God initiates covenant with all of creation,* as revealed in the earliest biblical stories of creation. One can almost imagine the early Jewish storytellers, explaining that God created each part of creation for different purposes, and each part needs the others. God gave the plants and trees to the people and animals for food (Genesis 1:29-30), and a river flowed through Eden to water the garden (Genesis 2:10). Human beings were placed in the garden to tend it (Genesis 2:15). Throughout the biblical witness, one finds story after story attesting to the covenantal relationship between God and creation, and among all parts of creation. In Exodus, a pillar of cloud provided protection, and God parted the sea so that the Hebrews could escape safely from slavery in Egypt (14:19-25). Much later, the stars in the sky and the waters of the Kishon River played a part in the victory of the Jewish people under the leadership of Deborah (Judges 5:20-21). These stories raise ethical questions about warfare, to be sure; but they represent the strong convictions of an ancient tribal people who were trying to make their way in the world. Their convictions were that God was the source of covenant and that the natural forces in God's creation were often working on their behalf; their lives were intertwined with the clouds and rivers and seas.

A second biblical theme is that *God's interaction with the creation is responsive.* In the first creation story, God delights in creation, and when God looks over it on the sixth day, God says that it is very good (Genesis 1:31). In the second creation story, God responds to Adam's need for companionship and creates another person, a woman (2:20-23). Later in this saga, we find God wrestling with Jacob through the night, finally blessing him and renaming him Israel (Genesis 32:22-32). We also find God responding to the wickedness of Nineveh by sending Jonah there to cry out against evil (Jonah 1:1-2). The story that unfolds is filled with God's responses: God responds to Jonah when he tries to run away from Nineveh (1:3-10), and God later repents the decision to destroy Nineveh after the people there repent (3:10). The same God talks strongly to Job when Job cries out about the calamities that have fallen on him and his family (Job 40:6–41:34). And we find Jesus lamenting over Jerusalem (Matthew 23:37-39). God is one who interacts with creation and feels the joy, pain, frustration, and hope that arise in the messiness of life. God feels and responds.

A third theme grows naturally from the first two, but it has often been forgotten in Christian history. *God is always present and active before people arrive.* Although the absence of God is sometimes noted in the biblical witness, the presence is a more dominant theme. Jonah, for example, finds that he cannot escape from God by taking a ship to Tarshish. God causes a big storm, and the sailors become frightened. When they discover that Jonah's unfaithfulness is the cause of this storm, they throw him overboard (Jonah 1:1-16). Jonah then spends three days and three nights in the belly of a big fish before he is thrown up on the shore and instructed once again to go to Nineveh. What is more, when Jonah finally goes to Nineveh and proclaims God's message, the people respond by repenting and the city is saved (1:17–3:10).

In this story, we find that God is always present, whether on a ship to Tarshish or in the city of Nineveh. In fact, Jonah cannot escape, even when he tries. Neither can the far-away city of Nineveh, for God is present enough to see their sin (1:2) and later to have pity (3:10).

When the absence of God is noted in the Psalms, it is often accompanied by a plea for God to respond to human cries (Psalms 10:1; 13:1; 22:1-2, 19; 27:9; 30:7; 35:22; 38:21; 44:24; 55:1; 69:17; 71:12; 88:14; 102:2; 143:7). Consider the familiar cry of Psalm 22, which is recited by Jesus from the cross: "My God, my God, why have you forsaken me?" (Psalm 22:1a; Matthew 27:46; Mark 15:34). These words reveal genuine experiences of God's absence. In each case, however, the story continues and God is found to be active still.[3]

The theme of presence raises critical questions regarding the missionary movements of more recent history. Missionaries from Europe and the Americas thought they were taking God to the native people of other lands. In the name of God, they often disrupted the lives of indigenous people, requiring them to live in missionary compounds—and sometimes labor very hard for political and military colonizers—and to give up their own religious and cultural traditions in order to become Christian. The Haida people of Canada were expected to give up their potlatches (festivals), and Pacific peoples were expected to abandon ancient practices of revering their ancestors. In some parts of the world, children were even removed from their families to live in mission schools or to be adopted by families who would raise them in the Christian faith and provide their education. Many Native American children in the United States and aboriginal children in Australia lost their family relationships and cultural roots as a result.

Although these acts were often well-intentioned, the intentions were easily distorted by unequal power relationships and unconscious assumptions of superiority. Some of the early attitudes and actions have since been repented and reformed, but an awakening of consciousness is still needed. Repentance and reform have sometimes been only partial, and sometimes superficial. The ability to demean other people, even unwittingly, is likely to continue in new forms whenever Christian people forget that God is always present and active before they arrive. African theologians have been particularly helpful in raising consciousness to this fact. Gabriel Setiloane argues that the supreme God *Modimo* was known by African people long before Christianity was born and many centuries before the eighteenth- and nineteenth-century Christian missionaries arrived.[4] A. Okechukwu Ogbonnaya echoes a similar theme and emphasizes that many formative theologians of the early church (such as Tertullian) were Africans.[5] In sum, God's presence supercedes human efforts to "bring God" to a people or a land.

Following this same theme, one can see that God is also present before we pray or call upon God. Our prayers make a difference to God, even opening possibilities for God and others to act in a particular situation.[6] At the same time, God's presence does not await our prayers. God's presence is a reality upon which we can depend. The very reality of God's presence encourages people to pray and respond with even more vigor.

Binding Communities

Another dimension of covenant arises from the stories of Holman Church and the partner churches in California and South Africa. These congregations all experienced a strong sense of community—not in the simple sense of warm feelings but in the vitality of being bound by a shared mission. As they worked together in mission, many warm feelings did arise, and their sense of community deepened. They themselves attributed the powerful bonds of community to God, and one binding experience opened into another. One could conclude that *God invites people again and again into deeper, more liberating, more empowering communal relationships.*

These relationships are not always smooth, but they are promising opportunities to walk with God and one another. They serve larger purposes as well; the stories reveal as much. Through covenantal relationships, even when conflict and misunderstandings arise, people are able to "make a way out of no way." This expression from the African American community is a strong reminder that covenantal relationships can empower people to do what seems impossible, to act on their highest values. If covenant communities serve only to make people feel good, that might be a good thing, but not good enough. Living in covenant community is sometimes difficult, but it serves *God's* good, and that *is* good enough. Covenantal living binds people together, opening the way for communities to be radically transformed as followers of Jesus.

Calling People to Action

The discussions of God's initiative and the communal nature of covenant already uncover another quality, namely that *covenant is always accompanied by God's call to action.* More is said of this quality in Chapters One and Two, but clearly the congregations of the two stories in this section reveal a strong sense of calling—callings that stirred immediate actions as well as continuing growth in new directions. Similarly, the biblical stories of covenant are filled with calls to action. Consider Adam and Eve, Jacob, and Jonah, just to name a few. All were expected to act in some way.

A call to action is rarely abstract; *the call is known amid the realities of life*—the realities of human and ecological interactions, with all of the cries and needs that are found there. In the two stories beginning this section, the realities of life were pressing. In the Los Angeles story, the realities were immediate; they required an urgent response. The Holman congregation was able to respond because the people were attuned to these realities. Further, the congregation itself had a long history of responding to the community, and individual members of the congregation had for many years been developing and using their gifts for others. In short, they were not ready for tragedy, but they were ready to respond.

In the second story, the realities of life were known in a very different way. A sense of call led the people of the Foothills suburban congregation to explore places of need. Only as they explored and listened carefully to people from other communities could their sense of call be connected fully and mutually with the two African congregations. They actively sought the guidance of others as they discerned their calling and prepared to respond. Their response was respectful and slow, allowing for careful preparations; thus, they adjusted their call to the realities they discovered. Their discoveries then inspired more discoveries and action by the Port Elizabeth congregation.

In addition to discovering calls amid the realities of life, *we often do not fully know a call until it unfolds over time.* Frequently I hear someone say, "Now I know why I was supposed to make this move or change in my life." Such a statement reveals that the person did not understand immediately where the earlier decision would lead and why it would be important. The purpose unfolded. Such unfolding does not necessarily mean that God had a full plan worked out in advance, although some would explain it in this way. The experience could also be explained as the way God meets people wherever they are and guides them to new paths, one step at a time. Whatever explanation of God's providence you choose, the congregations of this chapter experienced an unfolding of their calls. By taking one step along one path, the way was clear to take another step later.

These ideas lead back to the relation of call to covenant. *As a community's sense of call grows, so does its sense of covenant.* Such growth is what happened in the California congregations, and then in the South Africa congregation. Their initial responses led to further responses, but they did not know in advance where each step would lead. Neither could they have anticipated the powerful sense of communion with one another and with God that would grow in them as they responded. Such is covenant, which grows with call just as call emerges from covenant.

At the deepest level, *a call to action frees people.* It enables them to see what really matters, to focus their love, to dedicate themselves to something or Someone larger than themselves. As people respond to God's call, they enter a continual stream of losing and finding themselves; that is the mystery of life. No matter how God calls, whether explosively or gently, the response has to be worked out in daily fidelity, in ordinary life. Keeping focus amid the seductive values of the larger culture is a life task.

Pointing to the Future

This discussion of covenant and call reveals, finally, that *God's covenant always points to the future*. More is said of the future in Chapters Three and Four, but the future focus is clearly intertwined with other covenantal qualities discussed in this chapter. Covenantal living is not about accomplishments and completions, but about a long, winding, and mysterious walk with God that has no end. When God fulfills one promise, God makes another one. And when human beings make one response to God, they become aware of the possibility of another.

Further, *covenantal living can move people toward one another and to the natural world in an ever-deepening circle*. As noted earlier, it is not a private affair between God and individuals, or even between God and communities. It is a connectional reality. The congregations described in this chapter had diverse experiences, but their actions inevitably led them into deeper relationships with one another and the whole world around them. The Slovakia congregation described at the beginning of this chapter has become intensely aware of the issues in their country (issues for people, government, and land) as they have sought to support ministries throughout the region. Similar consciousness is stirred for the California and South Africa congregations. Sometimes the consciousness that emerges is actually a critique of the past consciousness of one's community. The practice of covenantal living does not guarantee a steady flow of goodness and righteousness; it simply offers the potential for increasing awareness and deepening relationships. It does not guarantee that fallible human beings will make the best decisions in any moment of time; it does open the way for making ethical decisions.

Whatever awareness emerges, the challenge is for people to act in ways that contribute to God's future. *Covenantal living is a call to justice and righteousness, and the very practice of justice and righteousness can contribute to further possibilities in the future.* The moments when people live most fully in covenantal relationship inspire further action, both in the people's own community and in others. The challenge is to practice covenantal living in such a way that we grow in awareness and commitment to give ourselves fully to God's call and the well-being of God's creation.

Conclusion

The purpose of this book is to engage people in discovering and responding to God's covenant and call, particularly as they point to the future church. More particularly, the purposes are to discern how God moves in and through communities of faith; to rediscover the concept and practice of covenant; to challenge patterns of theology that rely on simplistic categories and "either/or" choices (as between a spiritual or prophetic church); and to envision new ways to understand, structure, and practice ministry. To these ends, the explorations of covenant are drawn from currents in the contemporary world, biblical traditions, post-biblical Christian traditions, root traditions of The United Methodist Church, and ministries of living congregations.

The book is centered around three basic assumptions regarding identity and ministry: (1) Christian identity and ministry emerge as people live in covenant with God and one another amid the realities of the world; (2) both are grounded in the relational being and work of God; and (3) both invite people to participate in God's work in the world, however awkwardly or inadequately that may be expressed.

The first assumption is that the way a Christian community lives (with its heritage, commitments, and values) affects its self-understanding and practice of ministry. When this life is covenantal—even when the covenant is broken—people come to know themselves as bound with God, one another, and the larger world. The stories of this chapter reveal that a community's identity and its directions in ministry are like winding branches of ivy. Neither identity nor ministry is static, and neither is derived from the other; both are derived from the work of God's lively Spirit (the heart of the vine), which is constantly challenging, inspiring, and transforming the people of God.

The assumption that identity and ministry are derived from God leads to the second assumption: both identity and ministry are grounded in the God of relationships, who is revealed in the life, death, and resurrection of Jesus Christ and in the works of God throughout all time.

The third assumption invites people into God's work. It also invites them to look to living communities of the past and present for models of action, challenge, and hope. Even flawed communities can encourage and guide the walk of Christian disciples. All three assumptions, like branches of ivy, live always in relation to the vine, which is God.

Reading This Book

Exploring covenant and call—with their richness and complexity—is at the heart of this book. The chapters are designed for personal or group reflection, and each chapter includes resources at the end for meditation or further study and reflection. This book and others in the series are designed to stir conversation, provocative questions, and fresh vision in gatherings of church councils, committees, ministry teams, study groups, retreat communities, and so forth.

The Introduction has introduced the relationship between covenant and call. Chapter One includes an analysis of confusion and conflict that exist in the contemporary world, as well as insights regarding covenant and call that emerge in that world. Chapter Two is focused on God's covenant with broken communities, drawing largely on the biblical witness. Chapter Three builds upon Chapter Two, focusing on the diverse shapes of covenant communities over time, as seen in historical Christian communities. Finally, Chapter Four is an invitation to the future, looking to God's future for called communities. In the spirit of the Wesleyan tradition—seeking God in the witness of Scripture, tradition, experience, and reason—each chapter draws from all of these sources. Although some chapters draw more heavily on one, the sources are interwoven in hopes of illumining God and the ways of God for the church.

Each chapter includes (1) at least one congregational story, analyzed in relation to the theme of the chapter; (2) analysis, interpretation, and projections for the future; (3) a poem, hymn, or reading for meditation; and (4) questions for further reflection. While each chapter points toward action, the final chapter includes some specific proposals. As you read this book, you are invited to approach it as a partner in dialogue—reading, ruminating, questioning, meditating, and asking yourself and your community questions. The hope is not that you will agree with everything in these pages. The hope is that the Spirit of God is part of the writing and the reading. The hope, finally, is that your reading of this book will inspire and move you to transformed visions and actions.

Resources for Meditation

Meditate on moments when you have experienced God. Choose one name for God that is important to you. Meditate in silence, repeating this name again and again.

Meditate on "God of Many Names," a hymn written in 1985 by contemporary British composer Brian A. Wren. What responses are stirred in you as you consider the many names for God?

> God of many names, gathered into One,
> in your glory come and meet us, moving, endlessly becoming;
> God of hovering wings, womb and birth of time,
> joyfully we sing your praises, breath of life in every people,

> **Refrain:** Hush, hush, hallelujah, hallelujah!
> Shout, shout, hallelujah, hallelujah!
> Sing, sing, hallelujah, hallelujah!
> Sing God is love, God is love!

> God of Jewish faith, exodus and law,
> in your glory come and meet us, joy of Miriam and Moses;
> God of Jesus Christ, rabbi of the poor,
> joyfully we sing your praises, crucified, alive forever,
> **Refrain.**

> God of wounded hands, web and loom of love,
> in your glory come and meet us, carpenter of new creation;

God of many names, gathered into One,
joyfully we sing your praises, moving, endlessly becoming,
Refrain.

Questions for Reflection

• Recall a time in your life when you experienced yourself in covenantal relationship with God. What did you experience of God and
God's call? (Note: The time you recall may be a moment of intense
joy, or it may be a time of struggle or hardship.)

• Recall a time in your congregation when the community (the whole
congregation or a group within the larger body) experienced itself
in covenantal relationship with God. What did the community
experience of God and God's call? (Note: Again, the moment may
be a happy or difficult one; it may even be a moment with minimal
emotion or conscious awareness of covenantal bonding.)

Endnotes

1 From *Being As Communion: Studies in Personhood and the Church*, by
John Zizioulas; © 1985 St. Vladimir's Seminary Press; page 134. Used by
permission of St. Vladimir's Seminary Press, 575 Scarsdale Road, Crest-
wood, NY 10707.

2 From letter by Mary Lautzenhiser-Fraser, April 18, 1998. Used by permission.

3 The themes of absence and presence are often combined to emphasize
God's future, which is already here but not fully here. God's future will,
finally, be filled with God's presence. This theme of presence-absence can
be found in the second Temple period of Israel and in early Christian affirmations. In the latter, Jesus has departed but is still present and will come
again in fullness at the end of time.

4 See *African Theology: An Introduction*, by Gabriel Setiloane (Skotaville
Publishers, 1986); page 29.

5 See *On Communitarian Divinity: An African Interpretation of the Trinity*,
by A. Okechukwu Ogbonnaya (Paragon House, 1994).

6 See *In God's Presence: Theological Reflections on Prayer*, by Marjorie
Hewitt Suchocki (Chalice Press, 1996).

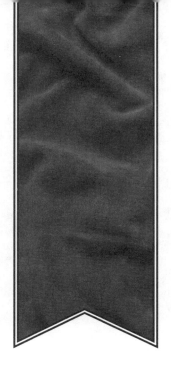

CHAPTER ONE

COVENANT AMID CONFUSION AND CONFLICT

Once upon a time, a lawyer asked Jesus what he should do to inherit eternal life. That is a good question. Jesus answered with another good question, "What is written in the law? What do you read there?" The lawyer had a handy answer to this question, "You shall love the Lord your God with all your heart, and with all your soul, and with all your strength, and with all your mind; and your neighbor as yourself" (Luke 10:25-27). This was an impressive answer, and this would have been a good place for the conversation to end. Jesus, in fact, answered, "You have given the right answer; do this, and you will live" (10:28). But this man had apparently learned to avoid dealing with answers by asking more questions. He turned to Jesus again and asked, "And who is my neighbor?" (10:29). Jesus answered with a story.

> Once upon a time, a certain man went from Jerusalem to Jericho. But the man fell among thieves, who stripped him and wounded him and almost killed him. A priest came by, and when he saw the wounded man, he passed on the other side of the road. A Levite appeared next. He looked but he also passed on the other side. Now a certain Samaritan was passing by, and when he saw the wounded man, he had compassion. He went to the man and bound his wounds, pouring on oil and wine. He put the man on his beast and took him to an inn where he cared for him. When the time came for the Samaritan to depart, he gave money to the innkeeper for the wounded man's stay, and he promised to return with more money if needed.
>
> (Luke 10:25-35, paraphrased)

Jesus ended his story with yet another question: "Which of these three, do you think, was a neighbor to the man who fell into the hands of the robbers?" (10:36).

In this simple conversation between Jesus and the man who wanted to inherit eternal life, a clear call is given for the man to love God and love his neighbor. The man is being called back to covenant with God, with neighbor, and with himself. Then the question is opened wide: Who is the neighbor, or with which people is this covenant to be enacted?

The story of the man who asked, Who is my neighbor? raises questions that local churches meet daily: Who are our neighbors, and with whom are we supposed to be in covenant? The purpose of this chapter is to wrestle with such questions. We will (1) explore some of the diverse ways that churches in the present world understand and live their call to covenant; (2) analyze some of the confusion and conflict in our contemporary world; and (3) draw conclusions regarding the call to covenantal living in such a confusing and conflictual world.

The story of the good neighbor puts forth a theme that is common in Luke's Gospel: the gospel message is for all, and it is found even in the most unlikely places. Jesus' message has to do with compassion. Luke often told shocking stories of marginalized people (sinners, poor people, outcasts, women) who were recipients of God's concern or witnesses to God's message. Luke repeatedly portrayed outcasts as part of God's covenant. In Luke's Gospel, we find stories of Elizabeth and Mary before Jesus' birth; the woman with the lost coin; the lost sheep; the prodigal son; Zacchaeus; and Jesus' forgiveness of the thief on the cross. In Luke's view, God's Word is not bound within a narrow, elite community. It is related to the Samaritan and the man beside the road, and who knows what others? Even more threatening in Luke, the embodiment of love and neighborliness is not limited to the Jewish and Christian communities either. In the story, the Samaritan, not the devout priest or the Levite, is the embodiment of love and neighborliness. Jesus tells the lawyer who is so full of questions to go and do like the Samaritan, the person in the story who has shown mercy. Is this the covenantal call?

Churches Living in Covenant

A local church in Nevada became alarmed about the crime that was destroying life in their city. The crime varied from drug dealing to violence against people and property to murder. The people of this church were frightened, especially for their children. They were also alarmed about the future of their church and city. In their deliberations, they talked with representatives of Boys and Girls Clubs of America and several other youth-serving agencies in the city, along with other religious communities. They discovered quickly that many others shared their concerns. Soon thereafter, they made a decision to host an after-school program for youth—a program in which many religious communities and youth agencies worked together to provide presence, fun, tutoring, and enrichment for young people of their city. The program grew to one hundred youth within the first two months.

This church in Nevada sees itself as a covenant community, connected with all of the people of their city and concerned about the confusion and conflict threatening youth around their church. When I first heard this story from the pastor, I commented, "You seem to be collaborating with many people to make a difference for youth." His response was enthusiastic, "Yes, *collaboration* is the key word; that is how we understand ourselves." This church sees its mission as collaborative, not only responding *to* the needs of many people, but also responding *with* many people. This is the spirit of covenant, recognizing one's own community as connected with all others, recognizing responsibility to others, and joining with others in responding to the cries of the world.

The church of this story was empowered into action by attending to what was happening all around them and by walking into the middle of their fear and concern. They prayed and talked with one another. They talked with many others. They made decisions for action. This community, in the midst of confusion and conflict, is able to celebrate and live covenantally—to live as a called people, following where they think God is leading them.

In the movie *Amistad* we encounter the story of a shipload of Africans who have been captured in their homeland to be sold into chattel slavery in the United States. The Africans rebel on the ship and later make efforts in United States courts to win their freedom. As the courtroom drama unfolds, one discovers the ambiguous role played by abolitionists throughout this case. Another drama has taken place outside the movie theaters, where some people argue that filmmakers distorted the picture of abolitionists. One argument is that filmmakers ignored the influence of Christian faith on abolitionists' positions, as well as the continuing influence of the Amistad Committee within Congregational churches and, later, the United Church of Christ. Formed in 1839, the Amistad Committee became the foundation for social-justice ministries in these churches, contributing to the formation of schools for freed slaves after the Civil War, support for the civil rights movement in the twentieth century, and many other justice ministries since then.

The events of the Amistad story suggest how complex are efforts by Christian people to live in covenant with their neighbors, and how easily their efforts can be misconstrued or belittled. Assuming that the motives of abolitionists were relatively pure, namely to love mercy and do justice, one can see that the Amistad event and actions that followed were a response of courageous people to follow their call from God. In so doing, they were living in covenant with God and with their African and African American neighbors. Even if the abolitionists' motives were mixed, as the film indicates, the people may still have been responding to their call, but doing so with the distortions and finitude of ordinary human beings. In either case, the critics' concerns about the movie's accuracy is important; the abolitionists at least had the courage to look into confusion and conflict and to respond to God's covenant and call in the midst of a messy and unjust world.

Confusion and Conflict

In the closing years of the twentieth century, much newsprint and computer paper is filled with discussions of contemporary global trends. If we could fly with the birds, we could look down on the global landscape and see very complex patterns. We would see patterns of mountains, lakes, highways, and byways, and patterns of war, poverty, abundance, and simple gestures of kindness. Much of what we would see from high altitudes would give hope that a new century is bringing new possibilities for good. We would see evidence of increased global communication, rapidly expanding knowledge, daily advances in technology, and ever-increasing possibilities for international interchange. We may, however, recognize dangers, especially those highlighted by Mercy Amba Oduyoye from Ghana, who observes that most global changes benefit the rich and do further damage to the poor. She says, "Today's tantalizing concept of globalization shows a face of unity that sucks the energies of all but nourishes the most economically powerful." [1]

However one evaluates globalization and social change, one fact is obvious: our neighbors are in easy reach. We would certainly see this reality if we flew with the birds. But like Oscar Wilde's gilded prince standing over the city, we would also see many sights to give us pain. The unhappy prince of Wilde's story saw a mother and child without food, a young writer without food or firewood, and many other sights that awakened his compassion. [2] We will see the same and more. We will see increased poverty and hunger, depleted resources, continuing fears of nuclear weaponry, and economic chaos. Further, we will notice that our neighbors are often behind barriers that we have helped build, barriers that are difficult to climb.

Most people and most communities have a preconceived mindset about the global situation and what needs to be done in ministry. They have a particular view of covenant and what Christians are called to do with their lives as they look at everything through that mindset. Like the priest and Levite, we pass by the beaten person because we have other things to do. Perhaps we think the church's ministry is preaching or social service or pastoral counseling. Perhaps we never even notice the needs outside our narrow mindsets; we never see the world with all of its particular needs. Perhaps the priest and the Levite in Luke's story also had a clear mindset about needs in the world and where they were called to serve. They scurried off to do their duties, hardly noticing the needs alongside their path and the call of covenant to respond to the wounded man.

Such narrowness is a reality for modern people as well. Consider my experience with a friend who serves a local church in a wealthy Southern suburb. When I first met this woman, I assumed that she probably had an easy existence and that most people in her immediate world had similar ease. One day I received this letter from my friend:

> My 81-year-old father was savagely beaten in his home by a 16-year-old boy last month. I spent most of the month in my hometown nursing him. The boy, a star wrestler on the school team, intended murder and is in great need of psychiatric help. The only way he can get that help on a long-term basis is to try him as an adult. Minimum penalty for a juvenile is 9 months; he needs 3–5 years to get his abused child syndrome worked out. My father is truly remarkable in that he fought for his life and won, although he bears some pretty bad injuries. The boy used a three foot lead pipe and stomped my dad's chest and neck.[3]

Neither my friend in her comfortable suburb nor her father in a small midwestern town was isolated. Problems of child abuse, crime, legal systems, and perhaps even race and class came down on them. My inability to see my friend outside of a stereotype impaired my ability to know myself in covenant with her until she cried out in this letter. Further, her own ability to appreciate the power of Christian forgiveness was stretched when her father later visited and forgave the boy who had attacked him, leading to a radical change in the boy's life.

Perhaps Christian people can begin simply by attending to the world that defies stereotypes and by helping others to attend. Attending can lead to responding, and to the hope that the person beaten along the side of the road will not be left to die. With that hope in mind, we turn now to some common dichotomies that are used to explain the world. A dichotomy is like a magician's wand that is waved to make things disappear. Of course, the magician's rabbit does not really disappear; neither does the reality that is waved away by a dichotomy. This discussion is intended to discourage people from using such dichotomies to oversimplify the world. Consider some of these.

Optimism and Pessimism

In a world of confusion and conflict, we are naturally pulled between optimism and pessimism. Youth in the United States often describe their lives as futureless, justifying self-destructive behavior such as drug-dealing with the argument that it is the only future they can see. Some of these same youth (and others) also express optimism that new knowledge and technology can help resolve the earth's problems, or they express optimism that they can do better in building a just and peaceful world than their parents and grandparents did. Such thinking might be partially influenced by developmental tendencies among youth to divide things into neat categories, but youth also live in a larger culture that encourages such oppositional thinking. In fact, much adult discussion about youth expresses the same dichotomies; youth are portrayed as dangerous and vulnerable, or as starry-eyed and hopeful. In fact, the realities of youth and adult worlds are far more complex than that. In mutual dialogue, youth *and* adults can help one another understand those complexities much better.

The pull between optimism and pessimism is evident in debates about whether resources are limited or limitless, or whether the space program drains money and attention from urgent social needs or leads to innovations in hospital care, weather monitoring, and human services. Further debates center on the increasing destruction of agricultural land for commercial purposes, the role of churches and countries in welcoming refugees, approaches to international debt, and shifts from traditional job patterns toward technological and informational services that displace some people while enhancing the work of others. In the midst of such confusing and conflictual issues, social change is real, and people often choose between an attitude of optimism and pessimism rather than engage the messy issues themselves.

The pull between optimism and pessimism is even present in local churches. We expect that technology will make it possible to minister to people more effectively through videocassettes, closed-captioned television, computerized membership records, and so forth. At the same time, we fear that technology could blind us to needs of real people and the earth. Declining membership in many churches contributes to pessimism, and lively new ministries contribute to optimism. Certainly, many people cite membership decline and doctrinal debates as reasons for pessimism within The United Methodist Church. Others look at the same issues and argue optimistically that new ministries could renew the church and that doctrinal discussions could enliven the church, even without doctrinal unity. The conflict between optimism and pessimism is alive and well in The United Methodist Church, as in other denominations.

As we consider the covenant and call of the church, we are tempted to choose naive optimism or equally naive pessimism. The optimistic choice can freeze people by giving a false sense of security that everything will be fine, that we do not need to act. The pessimistic choice can freeze people with a sense that nothing we do will make a difference, so we might as well do nothing. In either case, we will not act. We will not respond to the person by the side of the road. We will assume that the person will get well without our help or that our help will be useless because the person is doomed to die anyway. Beverly Harrison reminds the middle class of the world that pessimism is a luxury no one can afford.[4] Perhaps we can afford neither pessimism nor optimism! Hope emerges from neither;

hope is an honest facing of problems, combined with a trust in God's promise of new possibility.

Christianity and Secularity

Another common dichotomy, found in some countries more than others, is that of Christianity and secularity. This dichotomy is so common in North America that it is rarely questioned. For example, certain Christian churches do not allow "secular" music to be played in a wedding ceremony. More dramatically, part of the Christian schools movement is based on the assumption that "secular humanism" is diametrically opposed to Christianity, and that Christian schools are a necessary alternative to public schools, which are grounded in secularity. H. Richard Niebuhr has named this way of thinking about Christianity and secularity "Christ against culture."[5] The point of view is based on a central idea that secular belief or practice cannot be religious; it must be critiqued from the view of Christ.

This dichotomy, commonly accepted in the United States, Australia, and many parts of Europe, is not so easily presumed in many other parts of the world. In Kenya, where neither a state religion nor complete separation of religion and state has existed, the relationship between the secular state and religious communities has been one of partnership. According to the Kenya Education Commission Report (1964), for example, the churches and mosques are to provide religious education for conversion, salvation, and growth in faith, whereas the state schools are to provide religious education for growth of mind, body, and spirit. Further, Kenya's Education Act 1968 provides for religious instruction and worship in the schools, and it also allows parents to provide an alternative for their children if the religious education provided is not appropriate to their beliefs. This approach is possible because dichotomized thinking is not dominant in Kenya; religion and secularity are not seen as diametrically opposed.

David Martin, a British sociologist, believes that secularization is overrated as a stimulus for change in the modern world.[6] This is likely true, but secularization is still a fear-inducing phenomenon. For example, the controversies over prayer in the schools and over evolution vs. creationism still rage with great emotion in the United

States. Complicating the picture still more, issues of secularization get mixed with issues of privatized religion. The dichotomy between secularity and religion allows the public realm to be left to the "secular," pushing religion into the private realm of belief and practice. This dichotomizing movement has deep roots in history, but it has been radically questioned since the 1980's, when Martin Marty published *The Public Church,* bemoaning the problem of divorcing faith from the public world.[7]

In fact, the dichotomizing movement was questioned long before Marty published this book that introduced the now popular term *public church.* The very history of Methodism in Britain, Europe, and the United States is grounded in Wesley's idea of "social holiness."[8] In social holiness, public dialogue and action are seen as marks of Christian faith. Wesley himself wrote letters to government officials, sought out miners and other struggling poor, and publicly denounced slave-trading, to name only a few of his actions. How do United Methodists today engage the public world without dichotomizing Christianity and secularity?

Christianity and Other Religions

Another tension in the global context is between Christianity and other religions. Covenantal relations are magnified when we turn to peoples of diverse religious traditions. We as Christians are challenged to come together with Christians of all varieties—and with Jews, Muslims, Buddhists, and non-religious communities—in seeking the public good. After all, the Samaritan was the neighbor in Luke's story of Jesus. He would have been claimed neither by the Jewish listeners nor by early Christians. But God is not bound into our communities. We must find good ways to relate with people in other religious and cultural traditions.

The problem is represented by a woman who was offended by a children's curriculum resource that pictured an *Ojos de Dios* (the Eye of God symbol in some Mexican and indigenous art). She associated these symbols with native religions, which she believed had been rejected by Christianity. The woman's concern can be contrasted with that of the Catholic doctor from Nigeria who cannot understand why Muslims and Christians in Africa have such trouble in relating. "After all," he says, "they worship the same God." Now place these testimonies alongside the Native American Christian church in Arizona that had two sweat lodges on its side lawn for some time. The shaman who led worship in the sweat lodges and the minister who led worship inside the church cooperated in serving the needs of the Native American people in the community.

The relationship between Christianity and other religions is subject to many points of view, but the subject arouses intense emotions. In the past two thousand years, Christians have been persecuted, and they have been persecutors. Some of the bloodiest and longest wars in history have been religiously motivated and sustained. We should not wonder, then, that one tension on the contemporary global landscape is the relation between Christianity and other religions. What alternatives exist to dichotomizing? How might people from diverse traditions live respectfully and justly together?

Individuals and Communities

One final dichotomy to be considered here is that between individuals and communities. The pull between autonomous individuals and cohesive communities is pervasive in many corners of the world. The pull becomes dichotomized in the idea that a person is a separate being who can exist apart from society, and a society is a community that is minimally affected by the individuals forming it. The dichotomy puts forth a choice between individual and community needs, and between a chaos in which every person makes independent decisions (complete relativism) and a unity in which all decisions are made for the good of the community (universalism).

Such a dichotomy serves to oversimplify the tension rather than to address it. What would be more helpful would be a concept of the interrelatedness of individuals and communities. We need to recognize that individuals are formed in social interaction with people and communities that touch their lives. Likewise, societies are formed and transformed by individuals within and outside their group. A simple choice between the individual and community is not possible. Neither is it possible to choose between ministering in the private sphere and ministering in the public sphere. One permeates the other. In fact, Martin Marty points out that we need "to rediscover these two poles of existence," especially now when "the stakes are raised on both sides."[9]

The interconnection between individuals and social groups is obvious in many cultures where the dichotomy between individuals and communities does not play a major role. In most Native American, Asian, and African communities, such a dichotomy is contrary to the dominant worldviews. The African slogan, It takes a village to raise a child, is not just a fad; it is a long and deep tradition. At a picnic with a Native American church, you would likely discover that everyone cares for every child, and parents do not supervise and play with their own children any more than they supervise and play with others' children. Does this mean that these communities are not concerned with individuality? Certainly not! What it means is that individuality is thought to come from the experience of each individual in community life rather than from individuals' struggling against community influences.[10] Individuality is thus understood and formed differently than in communities where the dichotomy between individual and community is a more prominent way of thinking.

Cultures vary, but dichotomizing between individual and community introduces problems for most cultures. This is because people are influenced by their individuality and communality simultaneously, both for good and for ill. Consider some obvious examples. Consider how television influences individuals in their perspective on the world. Consider how individuals' feelings about sexuality and about life and death influence public movements on abortion. Consider how a person's family life shapes his or her beliefs, values, and passions. If family life is abusive, for example, aspects of that abuse live inside the person forever; if family life is gentle and respectful, aspects of that gentleness live on in family members. At the same time, individuals have shaping influence on communities, so patterns of abuse can be interrupted and reformed, even though residual feelings and values continue to play their part in peoples' lives.

This discussion suggests that the dichotomy between individuals and communities is false. As in the other dichotomies, it is an oversimplification. The dichotomy disguises the intricate relations among individuals and their communities, thus distorting the church's attempts to live in covenant.

Confusion and conflict in the contemporary world are real; any attempt to hide them with simplistic categories thwarts our ability to see the whole of reality and to live in covenant with the complex whole. In the following section, we consider challenges that the church faces in being called to covenant living.

Call to Covenant Living

The radical call to covenant in our new century is like challenges of ages past, yet complexities are multiplied dramatically. Christians are called to see, hear, and touch the world, and to respond with compassion and justice. God calls people into covenant with the larger world, even when we struggle to ignore the call, build walls to enclose ourselves, or belittle and dominate others. The challenge is to relate to the world in ways that are culturally appropriate and healing for one's own community and for others.

Relating with the world takes different forms, depending upon whether a community is under threat from the larger culture, is dominating others, or both. Some communities are threatened because of race, social class, or religious views. In many of these communities, people experience intense pain; they need a strong group to strengthen them for living well with the rest of the world. It is for these reasons that the health of African American, Hispanic (Latino), Native American, Vietnamese, Pacific-Island, and other ethnically-formed churches is so important.

For other people, pain is linked with narrowness more than with threats from outside. For them, genuine relationships with people beyond their group are urgently needed. As a result, strong relationships within and across congregations are critical. Also important are congregational programs to develop stronger relationships with one's city, town, or neighborhood. The challenge is that local churches usually discover many of these needs side by side.

In light of this complexity, what responses are needed? Certainly, Christian covenant and call take many forms. Ministry has to do with responding to God's call in the messy middle of a particular context and in relation to the larger world. If we take this challenge seriously, the confusion and conflict of our world might be met with covenantal responses. We are challenged to covenant with hope, to covenant with diverse cultures, to covenant with other religious communities, and to covenant with individuals and communities.

Covenant With Hope

A look at the dichotomy between optimism and pessimism suggests that neither is an adequate response to global complexity. A study of the tradition of covenant suggests that covenant is grounded not in our natural human proclivity to expect the best or the worst, but in a faithful relationship with God. Relating with God is itself grounded in hope—hope that God is present, that God feels the pain of the world, that God will act with compassion, and that God will continue to act until the end of time. Such hope offers no easy answers, but it does offer power.

In the case of the Nevada church described earlier, hope empowered the people to respond to youth in a situation that seemed hopeless. In the case of the Africans who protested their imprisonment on the Amistad, hope empowered the captives to fight, and it later empowered other people to support their legal struggle for freedom. Further, the hope born in the Amistad situation multiplied and empowered people to continue their work, founding schools and movements for social justice that have continued for more than 150 years.

Covenant With Diverse Cultures

Just as the dichotomy between optimism and pessimism is inadequate, so is the dichotomy between Christianity and secularity. Christian people need to realize that any division between the religious and secular is artificial at best. Religious values and beliefs permeate all culture; likewise, the larger dynamics of culture permeate religious communities and their practices. Further, multiple cultures exist, so one cannot assume a single religious tradition alongside a single cultural tradition. Most people live within multiple influences of religion and culture. The challenge, then, is to give the relationship between religion and culture, and between Christianity and culture, a deep analysis and critique rather than a simplistic dichotomy.

Further, the challenge is to join with other Christian communities in public discourse about issues of common concern. This is the work of collaboration. It is the work of a public church, a communion of communions. Martin Marty has focused on joining Catholics, mainline Protestants, and evangelicals, encouraging them to engage in public discourse and subject all views to the Word of God.[11] The purpose of such discourse is not just to get various groups to be friendly, and not even to press for agreement, but to address critical public issues such as education, media, and economic development in light of Christian commitments. In so doing, we often discover that so-called "secular" issues raise new questions for and insights into Christian faith. For example, economic shifts raise new questions about the meaning of life and the interconnectedness of life on the globe.

To suggest such a covenantal relationship among Christian communions is easier to say than to do. In very few local communities do such relationships exist. The challenge becomes even more strenuous when these communions of communions attempt to address critical public questions around which people have different views. If churches can actually build such covenantal relationships, they will be moving toward building a new way of being in the world.

Covenant With Other Religious Communities

This discussion leads naturally to another covenantal challenge, namely, to enter dialogue with other religious communities in order to foster better understanding of one another and to address common public concerns. Far from diverting Christians from their unique religious commitments, this kind of dialogue can actually deepen Christian commitments. Thomas Merton, for example, experienced the encounter with Indian religions as significant in deepening his Christian faith.[12] Similarly, John Cobb discovered after years of Christian-Buddhist dialogues that the natural result was to deepen commitments among both Christians and Buddhists.[13] Diana Eck discovered that people cannot share deeply and understand others unless they are willing to share their religious traditions.[14] These personal accounts suggest that relating with people of other religions is not only important for the sake of religious tolerance and peaceful human relations, but also for deepening one's own faith.

The examples of Merton, Cobb, and Eck may suggest a deceptive ease in relations among religions. In fact, interactions can be difficult; basic values and beliefs are brought into question. People are challenged by issues where agreement is forever evasive. On the other hand, the purpose of these relations is not agreement but respectful, loving, and just interactions. For this reason, difficult topics are important to the relationships so that respect can be honest and real. My trialogue group (Jewish, Christian, Muslim) found great benefit in discussing difficult texts from our respective scriptures; however, we engaged the texts only after meeting many months on less controversial topics. We discovered that relationships deepened as people were honest about challenges in their own traditions and areas of non-agreement across traditions.

This kind of interchange challenges people to move beyond dichotomies and to deepen relations with people in other religious communities; it also stirs hope for a more just and peaceful future. Such relations are not superfluous for Christian communities. The Christian covenant is marked by love for all people and hope for God's future; this compels a covenantal relationship with people in other traditions.[15]

Covenant With Individuals and Communities

The final challenge of this chapter is to be in covenant with individuals and communities. The challenge is to minister with individuals in relation to their communities, and to minister with communities as wholes while respecting the diverse individuals within them. The challenge is to help people know and act effectively within their communities, and to help social groups and institutions respond to the particular people who participate in them and are affected by their actions.

One concrete task is to help individual people be aware of their communities and to act in them with integrity. This includes critiquing the communities' values, beliefs, and practices. It also includes critiquing oneself in relation to those communities. A lawyer belongs to a family, a legal community, a client community, a church community, a city or town, a state, a region, a country, and a world. All of those communities interact in significant ways with the lawyer's life. All need to be critiqued, and all need the responsible action of the lawyer. The same is true for farmers, homemakers, shopkeepers, doctors, factory workers, business leaders, and everyone else.

Another concrete task is to help communities be aware of individuals and to act with integrity toward them. For example, when a local church is deciding how to minister with people in their surrounding neighborhood, the leaders of the church need to be sensitive to the particular individuals who will be served. This approach probably suggests that people in the neighborhood community need to participate in making and implementing the plans. It also means that the local church needs to be guided not only by what has been done before, or what is the latest fad in church service, or what the neighboring churches are doing, but also by what is important to the people who will be served. Similarly, a local church or agency that engages public issues in the larger community, such as television programming or health care, needs to be aware of the individuals who will be affected by particular actions and policies. Principles abstracted from real individuals and communities are usually defeating of the spirit of the service.

Conclusion

The world is more than a place to be fixed; it is home. The world is beautiful, warm, wounded, and afflicted with all kinds of destruction and injustice. It is the place where we see more than confusion and conflict; it is where we see God and all of the rich textures of God's creation. In the midst of God's world, we also experience covenant and God's call to covenant living. In the next chapter, we will dive deeply into the sea of Christian tradition to discern the promises of covenant for broken communities.

Resources for Meditation

The following hymn was written at the turn of the last century, stirred by the Protestant encounter with issues of United States society. It is marked by a strong consciousness of pain in the world and strong optimism about Christian responses and solutions. Both of these qualities marked the first decade of the twentieth century. We are only beginning to see the qualities that mark the first decade of the twenty-first.

Take time to meditate on the words of "Where Cross the Crowded Ways of Life," allowing the words and images to communicate with you, and allowing God's Spirit to reach you through them. Then spend some time analyzing the hymn. Reflect on the passions and hopes of the author. If you were writing a hymn today, what passions and hopes would you choose to express?

> Where cross the crowded ways of life,
> where sound the cries of race and clan,
> above the noise of selfish strife,
> we hear your voice, O Son of man.
>
> In haunts of wretchedness and need,
> on shadowed thresholds dark with fears,
> from paths where hide the lures of greed,
> we catch the vision of your tears.
>
> O Master, from the mountainside
> make haste to heal these hearts of pain;
> among these restless throngs abide;
> O tread the city's streets again,
>
> Till all the world shall learn your love
> and follow where your feet have trod,
> till, glorious from your heaven above,
> shall come the city of our God!

> By Frank Mason North, in *The United Methodist*
> *Hymnal*, number 427, verses 1, 2, 5, and 6.

Resources for Further Study

The following resources are suggested for study of the diverse cultural realities and issues faced by Christians in The United Methodist Church.

Each in Our Own Tongue: A History of Hispanics in United Methodism, edited by Justo L. Gonzalez (Abingdon Press, 1991).

Out of Every Tribe and Nation: Christian Theology at the Ethnic Roundtable, by Justo L. Gonzalez (Abingdon Press, 1992). Out of print, but you may be able to find a copy in your church or conference library.

Churches Aflame: Asian Americans and United Methodism, edited by Artemio R. Guillermo (Abingdon Press, 1991).

First White Frost: Native Americans and United Methodism, by Homer Noley (Abingdon Press, 1991).

Heritage and Hope: The African American Presence in United Methodism, edited by Grant S. Shockley (Abingdon Press, 1991). Out of print, but you may be able to find a copy in your church or conference library.

Methodism's Racial Dilemma: The Story of the Central Jurisdiction, by James S. Thomas (Abingdon Press, 1992).

Questions for Reflection

- Where in your world (region, city, town) do you see confusion and conflict? What are the greatest challenges that you and your church face?
- What might your church do to enter covenant with hope, with diverse cultures, with other religious communities, and with individuals and communities in their midst?

Endnotes

1 From "The Doctrine of Trinity as a Paradigm for Community and Power: Thoughts from African Women's Theology," by Mercy Amba Oduyoye; presented at Oxford Institute in Methodist Theological Studies, Oxford, England, August 1997; page 6.

2 See *The Happy Prince and Other Tales,* by Oscar Wilde (1888).

3 From letter by Naomi E. Mitchum. Used by permission.

4 See *Making the Connections: Essays in Feminist Social Ethics*, by Beverly Harrison, edited by Carol S. Robb (Beacon Press, 1985).

5 See *Christ and Culture*, by H. Richard Niebuhr (Harper & Brothers, 1951).

6 See *The Dilemmas of Contemporary Religion*, by D.A. Martin (St. Martin's Press, 1978).

7 See *The Public Church: Mainline—Evangelical—Catholic*, by Martin E. Marty (The Crossroad Publishing Company, 1981).

8 See examples of John Wesley's pleas for holy living in the following writings of John Wesley: "Journal from November 1, 1739, to September 3, 1741"; "A Blow at the Root, or Christ Stabbed in the House of His Friends"; Sermon 113, "The Difference Between Walking by Sight, and Walking by Faith"; Sermon 85, "On Working Out Our Own Salvation"; Sermon 91, "On Charity."

9 From *The Public Church: Mainline—Evangelical—Catholic*, by Martin E. Marty (The Crossroad Publishing Company, 1981); page 43.

10 With research colleagues, I have discovered marked cultural differences in understandings of individuality and community, drawing upon ethogenic research of six congregations. Two of these studies have been analyzed in some depth in relation to the individual-community theme in "Dynamics of Religious Culture: Theological Wisdom and Ethical Guidance From Diverse Urban Communities," by Mary Elizabeth Mullino Moore, in *International Journal of Practical Theology*, Vol. 2, 1998; pages 240–262.

11 See *The Public Church: Mainline—Evangelical—Catholic*, by Martin E. Marty (The Crossroad Publishing Company, 1981); pages 3–22.

12 See *Thomas Merton: Social Critic*, by James Thomas Baker (The University Press of Kentucky, 1971); pages 118–123.

13 See *Beyond Dialogue: Toward a Mutual Transformation of Christianity and Buddhism*, by John B. Cobb, Jr. (Fortress Press, 1982).

14 See *Encountering God: A Spiritual Journey from Bozeman to Banaras*, by Diana L. Eck (Beacon Press, 1993).

15 These points are developed further in "Theological Education by Conversation: Particularity and Pluralism," by Mary Elizabeth Mullino Moore, in *Theological Education: Theory and Practice in Theological Education*, Vol. 33, No. 1, Autumn 1996; pages 31–47.

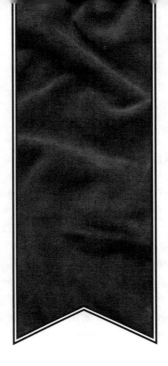

CHAPTER TWO

GOD'S COVENANT WITH BROKEN COMMUNITIES

In the previous chapter we explored some of the confusion and conflict in our contemporary world, and we drew insights from that world for covenant living. In this chapter, we turn to some of the brokenness in creation and the ways in which God's covenant actually arises in the midst of brokenness. Much of the pondering in this chapter is focused on biblical texts, but we begin with a story that uncovers both brokenness and possibility. The story provides a case for reflecting on call and covenant in relation to brokenness, and for connecting biblical worlds with the contemporary one.

This story of broken realities is told in first person, for that is how I experienced it. At the same time, the story points to thousands of other realities that happen with others every day. The first part of the story involves my initial relationship with a colleague from Hungary, and the later parts are the telling of later developments in that relationship.

Broken Realities—A Story

Several years ago, I attended an international theological institute where I met Antonia. Antonia was a United Methodist pastor in eastern Hungary, where she served a house church and did some teaching in the seminary several miles away. When I first met Antonia, I was committed to feminist movements in the church and was distressed about the oppression of women in local churches, theological schools, and international associations. In the particular institute where we met, I was grateful to be able to participate, but I was painfully aware of the near invisibility of people, especially women, from the Southern Hemisphere.

With such pressures bubbling inside me, Antonia's opposition to these same concerns bothered me. Further, Antonia was a strong character, who spoke often and with great conviction. Much of what she said was diametrically opposed to what I believed and valued. She was probably thinking the same of me. During the eleven-day meeting, I made a few gestures to get to know Antonia, but mostly I listened to her and let frustration build inside me.

About eighteen months after that meeting, I received a call from my bishop. He wanted a favor. The bishop had never asked a favor before, so I was prepared to respond. Then I learned what the favor was to be. Antonia was coming to California, and he wanted me to entertain her and help her itinerate and preach throughout the region while she was here. My heart sank. The bishop had been hosted by Antonia while in Hungary, and because he was to be away when she arrived, he wanted me to do the same for her. I wanted to respond to the bishop, but entertaining and traveling with Antonia seemed like an enormous challenge. Further, this was coming at the close of our school year, when I was fully loaded with responsibilities.

I said yes.

Before proceeding with this case story, we reflect briefly on the dynamics of the situation. First, I met Antonia because both of us were part of a connectional church—one that sponsors global meetings and sends bishops and others for visitation in different parts of the church. We were also part of United Methodist connections in our own locations—in local churches, districts, annual conferences, jurisdictions, and a myriad of networks. Because of these connections, Antonia wanted to visit California, and I felt compelled to say yes to the bishop. Because of our United Methodist connections, the churches and groups I asked to welcome our visitor said yes to me as well.

The connection was clearly not grounded on personal compatibility; it was not even grounded on obligation. It was grounded instead on bonds of community that transcend personalities and obligation, taking root deep inside of people. Antonia and I had both experienced bonds of connectional community in our own lives; these had led us into the meeting situations in the first place. The connections in our different parts of the world had helped nurture us into the distinctive individuals we were. The church connection also functioned between us, even when personal harmony was minimal and obligation could play only its small part.

In light of this discussion, one could say that the United Methodist connection is much deeper than surface relationships; it points toward *koinonia*, or sharing fellowship, which is finally a gift of God. Such a vision can be quite hopeful for The United Methodist Church today, especially when people wrestle with whether the church can fully accept its own diversity—diversity in theology, ethnicity, sexual orientation, social class, and region. The vision suggests that fellowship is not bound by sameness; it is strong enough to hold people who are quite different from one another.

These ideas run very deep in United Methodist and Christian traditions. In fact, the biblical and ecumenical visions of *koinonia* are closely akin to the connection of the early Methodist movement. Brian Beck believes that the word *koinonia* is richer than the word *connection* because it is more fully grounded in the Trinity (the trinitarian community within God). Also, *koinonia* embraces the fullness of unity and diversity rather than shunning diversity in order to preserve unity. At the same time, Beck argues that the early Wesleyan connection was a significant, embodied reality; thus, critical reflection on its structures of communion and accountability can suggest how *koinonia* might be more fully embodied in the modern church.[1] Both in the early church and in the early Wesleyan movement, the *koinonia* made social survival possible, and it nourished people in their faith. The whole concept of *koinonia* challenges people today to embody the ideal of sharing community. When *koinonia* is part of our lives, it supports our survival and nourishes our faith just as it did for the people in the early church and in the days of Wesley.

Challenges in Brokenness

The practical question posed by the preceding analysis is: How might the story of Antonia and myself have embodied *koinonia* more fully in the biblical sense? With that question in mind, we return to the story.

In the height of my anguish about Antonia's proposed visit, I had responsibility for introducing one of my classes to the process of doing case study analysis. The idea was for students to write brief case studies from their ministries, to analyze the situations with their colleagues, and to make decisions for future action. The students were nervous about this assignment, so I prepared an example. I wrote a short case study of the situation with Antonia, appending a list of questions for future practice. I invited the group leaders of the class to be my peer group, exemplifying the reflection process for the larger class; they were to analyze the case study and help me discern next steps.

One of the group leaders was a very strong feminist woman in the doctoral program in pastoral care and counseling. When the small group began their analysis, they identified many of the dynamics that I myself had identified. Then the woman in the group said that something else concerned her in this case. She described the ways in which women's communities often are torn apart by different perspectives within them. She described how women are often marginalized in the church and in other contexts, and how the women are further marginalized by a lack of solidarity among women. She concluded that a step toward building friendship or collegiality was needed in the case I had presented. The class was shocked, as were other members in the analysis group. People wanted to argue that this was a fruitless venture, for previous efforts to befriend had met with no response. I was not shocked. I knew that this analysis was very perceptive; I knew that I needed to find a new way to respond to Antonia.

One thing that was very clear to me in my saga with Antonia was that she and I were very different. If we were to be bound in *koinonia,* we needed to find a glue that was much stronger than theological agreement and much deeper than similar personalities. Further, the pressures of women's movements across the world, and increasing critiques of the white, North Atlantic, middle-class biases in the 1980's feminist movement, suggested that all solidarity among women needs to be grounded on more than agreement and personality. Both Christian faith and women's movements for liberation were demanding a new approach to difference. They were demanding more than shunning people who were different, or trying to change people with different views. In the case of Antonia and myself, we were both challenged to approach our relationship in a new way. The question was, How?

New Possibilities

We did not have to wait long before the opportunity for new approaches presented themselves. The very fact that I had said yes to the bishop's request and had taken the case study to my class for reflection revealed some degree of openness (or craziness) on my part. The fact that Antonia had said yes to the bishop's invitation and had prepared to share authentically in her preaching and teaching revealed some degree of openness on her part. The ground was cultivated, but much was still left to be resolved. Thus we return to the story one more time.

Several weeks passed. I was making final preparations to greet Antonia, having arranged preaching and speaking opportunities, as

God's Covenant With Broken Communities   51 *well as small group consultations with Antonia. Mostly, my husband, children, and I were planning to entertain her by showing her the region and welcoming her into our home and family life.*

When Antonia arrived, she was ill, having been in a strenuous meeting for almost two weeks and having lived with some oddities of United States culture (like ice in drinks) that did not agree with her well. We found ways to care for her, and she found ways to muster strength and participate in most of the planned activities. Mostly, we sat in our living room and visited, and we drove around southern California to some of the scenic and cultural sights of the region. Throughout this time we talked and talked, coming to know one another more deeply with each passing day. We came to admire Antonia's zeal and her care for her small house church. She seemed to feel at home with us as well.

During her stay, Antonia purchased a gift for every person in her small church, often buying clothes that they needed as well as tokens they could enjoy. She carefully selected just the right thing for each person. We also heard Antonia's story of faith as she preached and spoke in various churches. She took so much interest in our children that they stayed in the living room to visit long after good manners would have permitted them to leave. In the space of a week, we had become friends with Antonia. We delighted in her company; we could even discuss issues on which we disagreed. We came to understand what stood behind our differences, even to respect the differences.

Two years later, our family had the wonderful opportunity to visit Hungary, where we took a train to the eastern town where Antonia lived. We spent a full day as her guest, seeing her church (which was also her home), meeting church members, visiting sights in the region, eating Hungarian foods, learning Hungarian ways, and talking, talking, talking. We learned how people traveled several miles to worship each week, how Antonia converted her bedroom to a Sunday school classroom, and how people loved to sing. We also learned that members of Christian churches in Hungary were restricted from certain kinds of jobs; this was the last year of communist occupation and tight restrictions on Christian churches. Antonia glowed as she told us, however, that the Christian young people were especially wanted for jobs that involved caring for others. For exam-

Covenant and Call

ple, schools for children with special needs were staffed mostly by Christian teachers; these young adults had special gifts in working with the children.

When we parted from Antonia late that night, we were overflowing with gratitude and love. In her typically generous way, she gave each of us a gift—a sample of Hungarian culture that had been carefully selected for each one of us. We said our good-byes, making plans for our next meeting two years later. Two months before Antonia was scheduled to arrive in the United States, however, she died in her sleep. We had lost a very dear friend.

I have told this story in some detail because it reveals something of the yearnings and difficulties in human relationships. It reveals how a connectional church, like The United Methodist Church, brings unlikely people together. It reveals how simple differences make relationships awkward at times, and how larger dynamics of difference—nationality, race, culture, theological orientation, and personal history—can make those relationships even more awkward. At the same time, it reveals how issues brewing in the larger world, such as conflicts within movements of women and pressures exerted on women, have their effect as well. The brokenness in one relationship almost never stands alone; it is inextricably bound to the larger dynamics of culture, including church cultures. In short, broken realities are real, and we are challenged almost every day of our lives to mend brokenness, or to live with it as best we can. In the midst of these broken realities, we are met by the challenges of covenant and call.

Broken Realities—Biblical Stories

Broken realities are not unique to the modern world. The Bible overflows with stories of broken people trying to mend their brokenness or to live with it as best they can. The remainder of this chapter focuses on selected biblical texts. The primary focus is on covenant and implications for ministry, relating the biblical texts to the foregoing case and to one another. The texts are not addressed as simple stories with singular messages, but rather are analyzed in relation to their complexity and the human yearnings revealed through them. Attention is given to the confusion and conflict, as well as the hope and challenge, revealed in the texts. Though the analyses are brief, they set the stage for a final section of interpretation that draws parallels between the conflictual issues of the biblical communities and those of contemporary communities, seeking insights for covenantal living in relation to brokenness.

The following sections focus on four covenant stories in relation to human yearnings in a broken world, each story uncovering a basic picture of covenant. The story of God's covenant with creation (Genesis 1–2) reveals that covenant is grounded in God's relation with creation. The story of God's covenant with Noah (Genesis 9) reveals that God's covenant is with the whole earth and all who live on it. The story of God's covenants with Abraham, Sarah, and Hagar (Genesis 16–17) reveals that God's covenant promises a future, both to Abraham and Sarah's people and to Hagar's people. And the story of Jesus' last supper and last moments with his disciples (Luke 22:7-28) reveals that the new covenant in Jesus promises restoration of that which is broken in the world. Since we focused on creation stories in the Introduction, we attend to those briefly here and give more attention to the other three narratives.

Yearning for Life—Covenant Grounded in Creation

The focus in the Introduction was on three features of covenant, drawing particularly from Genesis 1 and 2. Covenant was identified as initiated by God, accompanied by a call to action, and pointing to the future. One can only imagine the power of these covenantal themes for early Jewish communities who were seeking a home, identity, and well-being in their ancient Mesopotamian world. They were likely overwhelmed by the graciousness of this covenant-making God, and surely they were also overwhelmed by the demands of God and the challenges upon them to be faithful. Whatever the particular feelings at a particular moment in time, the stories of the Covenant-maker gave them an anchor as they journeyed through the chaotic seas of life.

This anchor of covenant offered reassurance in many forms.

The people were reassured that God was their God and the God of all creation. They were reassured that God initiates covenant with creation, thus removing primary responsibility for the functioning of the world from their shoulders. They were reassured that God was responding to them at every turn—creating, protecting, observing the joys and hardships of their lives, and responding with comfort, challenge, and guidance. They were reassured that God is present and active in all situations, even before the people cry out. They were reassured that God invites the people into faithful and empowering relationship with God, one another, and the rest of creation. With such reassurances, the people were being told that they could depend on the trustworthiness of God. Further, the creation narratives offered explanations and limitations to circumscribe their lives, as well as guidance for daily living in their community.

Yearning for a Good Earth—
Covenant With the Whole Earth

One of the persisting tensions in most religious communities is the question of how much the faith of one people is limited to that people and how much it can be generalized to all people. This is a particularly live issue in the contemporary world where religious wars are stirring in every corner. The murder of twenty-eight people in Omagh, Northern Ireland, reveals the degree to which brokenness reigns. This incident in August 1998 took place within months after a vote that moved toward settlement of longstanding issues, yet this particular incident had more casualties than any previous paramilitary act in the region. The reality of brokenness echoes still, even after time has passed and people from Ireland and the United Kingdom have made much progress toward peace and well-being. The reconciliation efforts continue, even after centuries of animosity and brokenness between the two countries and between disparate groups of people within each country.

Similar scenarios are played out in tensions between the United States and Iraq, and between Israel and Palestine. In a much smaller way, the issue of religious difference became a point of disagreement between Antonia and myself. For Antonia, living in a communist situation with tight controls on Christian churches, the strong value of Christianity was important to emphasize. For me, living in a country strong in global power, being open to other traditions was important as well.

Within theology and the philosophy of religion, the debate has been framed by the three basic options offered by John Hick and Paul F. Knitter. They suggest that religious communions can choose among the exclusivist, inclusivist, and pluralistic options. Christian exclusivists claim that their view of the truth is true and that God's blessings are intended exclusively for followers of Jesus Christ. Christian inclusivists also claim that their view is true. They further believe that people of other faiths are loved and blessed by God, although these people experience and name the world in different ways. The inclusivists often argue that people relate to God through their distinctive faith traditions, but that other people worship the same God whom Christians know in Jesus Christ. Christian pluralists claim that their view of the truth is one among many; therefore, pluralists can share their faith commitments with others while receiving what others share as well.[2]

The purpose here is not to elaborate a position on these options but to urge people to know that options do exist. Whatever their distinctive perspective, Christians are challenged to love God through their distinctive faith tradition while valuing and respecting other people and their traditions. This valuing is more likely found in inclusivist and pluralist positions, but the more critical issue is an ability to see the yearning for God's whole earth and all of God's people that is at the heart of biblical witness. Further, the critical issue is to respond to God's creation with love and justice. This view is at the heart of Christian traditions, however varied they may be.

With these issues in mind, we turn to Genesis 9:1-17, the covenant told through Noah. The time came on the earth when "the earth was corrupt in God's sight, and the earth was filled with violence. . . . for all flesh had corrupted its ways upon the earth" (6:11-12). The scene was set for God to act, and as the story goes, God instructed Noah to prepare for a great flood by building an ark to certain specifications. Then Noah was to take aboard the ark his family and pairs of every living thing, of all flesh (6:13–7:10). For forty days and nights the rains fell, and the earth was flooded. And when the flood waters began to subside, Noah sent out a dove three times. The dove returned the first time without having found a place to land, returned the second time with a newly plucked olive leaf, and did not return the third time. Noah then knew that the water had subsided enough to go forth, and he led all of the families of creation off the ark (7:11–8:19).

Safe on dry land, Noah built an altar and made a sacrifice to God. Smelling the pleasing odor, the Lord then promised "in his heart" never to curse the ground again because of wayward humanity, and never again to destroy every living creature (8:20-22). This said, God's words to Noah and his sons are a familiar refrain, "Be fruitful and multiply, and fill the earth" (9:1). God emphasized the relation between humans and animals, with a renewed reminder that animals and plants are for humans to use, and with instructions for people to follow certain rules in relating to animals, plants, and other people (9:2-7). At this point, God renewed the covenant with Noah and his sons. This second time, the covenant was made in an expansive way:

> "As for me, I am establishing my covenant with you and your descendants after you, and with every living creature that is with you, the birds, the domestic animals, and every animal of the earth with you, as many as came out of the ark. I establish my covenant with you, that never again shall all flesh be cut off by the waters of a flood, and never again shall there be a flood to destroy the earth." God said, "This is the sign of the covenant that I make between me and you and every living creature that is with you, for all future generations: I have set my bow in the clouds, and it shall be a sign of the covenant between me and the earth."
> (Genesis 9:9-13; see also 9:14-17)

In several ways, this is a circular story; it circles back to themes that arise throughout the Hebrew scriptures. A first thematic circle is *God's awareness of evil in the world*, which reminds the reader of many other times when God regretted evil and sought to punish people or call them to faithfulness. In the Introduction we discussed the Jonah story; God is revealed there as responsive to evil in the world (in Nineveh and in Jonah's running away) and present in every situation before key people arrive. God's concern about evil appears again in the Noah story. A second thematic circle comes forth in *God's explicit instructions* to Noah on how to build and load the ark. God similarly gave specific instructions to Abraham, Hagar, Isaac, and Jacob—a recurring theme in the Bible. A third thematic circle is uncovered in the very structure of the story; the structure reveals what is now a very familiar form of covenant in the Scriptures. *God responds to something happening in the world; God promises an action and asks certain people to participate in it (Noah in this case); God's action is completed; people kneel to worship; and God responds yet again to the people at worship.* This covenantal cycle circles through Scriptures, although the variations are many.

The Noah covenant story is circular in some other ways that are internal to the story. *The flood story, which began with God's seeing evil in the world, closes with God's smelling the pleasing odor from Noah's sacrifice.* God's despair and delight frame the story. In both cases, God asks Noah and his family to participate in the divine work in particular ways. *God made covenant with Noah at the beginning of the story in giving instructions for building the ark (Genesis 6:14-16), and God again made covenant with Noah and his sons at the end with instructions for relating with animals and all creation (9:8-17).* Here the paired covenants accentuate the expansiveness of the second one, which is spoken to Noah *and* his sons, includes "every living creature that is with you," and extends to a promise that God will never again destroy the earth and all creatures in a flood. In Genesis 8:21-22 the promise is even more expansive and does not narrow the means of destruction to a flood.

One more internal circle is *the circle of promises and instructions.* At least three such circles are found in the story. First, God promises a punishing flood and instructs Noah to build an ark (6:9–7:10). Second, God promises "in his heart" never to destroy every living creature again (8:21-22) and instructs Noah and his sons to "be fruitful and multiply" and to relate with creation in particular ways (9:1-7). This particular promise-instruction also circles back to the Genesis 1 covenant story (1:28-30) and to other instructions to humans about their relations with animals (2:18-20; 3:1-6, 13-15, 21;

6:7, 20). Finally, God promises covenant with Noah's family and descendants and promises never again to destroy the earth by flood (9:8-17). This promise is followed not with instructions to the people but with a commitment from God to remember this promise whenever a bow appears in the sky (9:12-17). The implicit instruction is for the people simply to trust in God to keep the promise.

Just as the creation stories offered the people hope and guidance, so also did the flood story. The trustworthiness of God appears throughout the story, but particularly in the final promises. The wholeness and value of creation is affirmed, and human responsibility is underscored yet again. Certainly the yearning for a good earth is shown to be valued by God. God promises to honor this value in some particular ways (as in not flooding the earth again), and people are called to seek goodness for creation. Whether reaching out to Antonia or working for peace in Northern Ireland, people are called to care and to act.

Yearning for a Legacy—Covenant for Future

Another promise travels with covenant in the Bible; this is the promise of a future. The longing for a future, or a legacy, is strong in human nature. People often give birth and rear their children with hopes that their children can contribute well to the future. People often work hard in their jobs or volunteer work for the same reason. At the center of Jewish and Christian covenantal theologies is the hope for a good future, a future that represents God's new creation or kingdom. Long ago, Jürgen Moltmann wrote that in the Bible, God never fulfilled one promise without making another one.[3] This simple idea is very important to the covenant-making God.

Nowhere is the covenant for future more vivid than in the familiar story of Abraham and Sarah. What is often less familiar is the parallel promise that God made to Hagar.[4] The parallel stories begin with God's promise to Abram and Sarai that they would have children; they were to be blessed with many heirs (Genesis 13:14-18; 15:3-6). As the story goes, God walked with Abram and Sarai for many years without making good on that promise. The scene was

God's Covenant With Broken Communities   59 set for Sarai and Abram to take the covenant of future into their own hands (16:1-16). Since Sarai had borne no children, she had an idea for completing God's promise with her own initiative, using her Egyptian slave-girl Hagar. She said to Abram, "You see that the Lord has prevented me from bearing children; go in to my slave-girl; it may be that I shall obtain children by her" (16:2a). After ten years of living in Canaan and pondering the future, Abram was given Hagar as a wife. The gift came from Sarai. Abram went to Hagar and she conceived.

When Hagar realized that she had conceived, she looked with contempt on Sarai. Disturbed, Sarai said to Abram, "May the wrong done to me be on you" (16:5a). She complained that Hagar looked upon her with contempt, and prayed that the Lord would be judge between Abram and herself. Abram reminded her, "Your slave-girl is in your power; do to her as you please" (16:6a). Sarai dealt with the young pregnant girl harshly, and Hagar ran away. Now, the angel of the Lord saw Hagar running and called her by name. He asked where she had been and where she was going. When she explained, the angel told her to return to Sarai and submit. The angel also made a promise: "I will so greatly multiply your offspring that they cannot be counted for multitude" (16:10). Further, the angel also told Hagar that she would have a son, and that she was to name him Ishmael (God hears). She was told more, so much more that she named the Lord El-roi (God who sees). Then Hagar returned to Sarai as the angel had requested, and she bore a son. Abram named the child Ishmael.

In this story the young Hagar was used by Sarai and Abram for their own purposes; and the unborn child, Ishmael, became a refugee with his mother. In the midst of their plight, God heard and saw, revealing responsiveness yet again. What is even more surprising is that God made a promise to Hagar, paralleling the promise to Abram. In the ancient world, such action would have been considered most unusual. This text is the only place in Hebrew scriptures where God speaks directly to a woman, and the woman was an Egyptian slave-girl. Yet God spoke directly to Hagar with promises of many descendants. Hagar, as well as Abram and Sarai, were to have a promised future: many descendants from whom would come a great nation. Hagar returned to Sarai as she had been told to do, and her child was born.

In the story thus far, we find several covenantal themes echoing the themes of earlier biblical texts as well. The "be fruitful and multiply" theme of Genesis 1 (1:22, 28; see also 1:11-12) is echoed by the promise to Abram, and then to Hagar, for many descendants. When we consider these texts alongside Genesis 1, we see that *God covenants for an abundant future with all plants and animals and people of the earth.* Implicit in God's promises to Abram, for example, is the plenitude of creation. The multitude of stars in the sky and specks of dust on the ground will be mirrored in the plenitude of human offspring. Consider that these stories were being told in a world where life was strenuous and tenuous; early death was a grave reality. The focus was not on overpopulation (a modern problem), but on God's promise to keep the earth and human family alive through the hardships of daily living. Many peoples in the modern world feel these same pressures, which makes population control a challenging issue understood differently by people in different cultural communities and parts of the world.

Another echoing theme in the stories of Abram, Sarai, and Hagar is that *the covenant is made not with one person at a time but with a whole people.* Further, *God's covenant is not only with Jewish people but also with people who would descend from Hagar.* We find here an echo of the Noah covenant—a covenant with the whole world and with all peoples of the world. Here, as in the Noah story, the promise is not only for an abundant future, but also for protection. God is not promising an easy path (Genesis 16:12), but some form of presence and protection, even to Hagar's child. The covenant pushes here toward universal claims for God's relation with the world, although its clear attention is given, as we might expect, to the people whose story these Scriptures tell. The tension between a universal covenant and a distinctive covenant with Israel is made even more explicit in God's renewed promise to give Abraham and Sarah a son, to make covenant with their son Isaac, and also to bless Ishmael and his descendants (17:15-22). Both sides of the tension remain as the saga continues. With this, we return to the story.

God's Covenant With Broken Communities

As the story continues, Abram and Sarai, now called Abraham and Sarah, finally did have a child (many years after Ishmael was born). Isaac grew well, and when he was weaned (which might have been at about three years old), Abraham gave a great feast. At the feast, Sarah saw Ishmael playing with Isaac, and she was not pleased. Sarah told Abraham to cast out Hagar and Ishmael because Ishmael should not be allowed to inherit along with her son. Abraham sent Hagar and Ishmael away with nothing but some bread and a bag of water. Hagar and her son left, but they stopped and cried out when they ran out of water. God heard Ishmael and responded. God promised that Ishmael would have many descendants, and God showed Hagar where she could find a well. The covenantal promise was thus renewed with Hagar, Ishmael, and their descendants, as with Abraham and Sarah.

In light of this complex story, we see God still as a covenant-making God, and we also see God as entering covenant with multiple peoples. In an ancient tribal society, this thrust to recognize the universal covenant of God is quite surprising. For natural reasons, this is not the major thread of covenant tradition in the ancient texts. In the ancient world, each tribe was generally content to let other tribes be faithful to their own deities. The promise to Hagar and Ishmael is, however, a thread that acknowledges the continuing faithfulness of God, even to those who are cast out by the ancestors of the Israelites in whose book the story is told. We find here the wideness of God's mercy, the depth of God's compassion, and the fullness of God's covenant. We also find here the promise of a future to Hagar and Ishmael's people, as to Abraham and Sarah's.

Yearning for New Life—Covenant for Restoration

One other feature of covenant in the biblical witness is the promise of restoration. One finds this promise in many Hebrew Bible texts as well as in the New Testament. The focus here is on the last supper that Jesus celebrated with his disciples. In the Gospel of Luke, many theological questions, tender moments, and earth-shaking predictions precede this Last Supper. The theological questions include questions about Jesus' authority, paying taxes, resurrection, and Jesus' identity (Luke 20:1-44). Following such weighty questions is the moment when Jesus praises the significance of a poor widow's small offering of all she has (21:1-4). In the very next breath, Luke enters a description of Jesus' earth-shaking predictions: the destruction of the Temple (21:5-19), the destruction of Jerusalem (21:20-24), and the coming of the Son of Man (21:25-36). All of this leads to the Last Supper—a covenant meal celebrating Passover and preparing for Jesus' death (22:7-38).

In this brief glance at the literary setting of the Last Supper, one can see the cosmic significance of this event. One can also see some persisting themes that light the reader's way to the meal, just as surely as a streetlight shines on a roadway. In Luke's two preceding chapters, some key themes are emphasized: God's judgment, God's future that will still come, and the call on human beings to give (the widow's offering) and to be prepared for the coming "Son of Man" (21:34-36). In these themes are echoes that have already been sounded in the Genesis texts discussed earlier, as well as in the themes from Luke discussed in Chapter One. With this preparation, we turn to Luke's story.

The story unfolds on the day of unleavened bread when Jesus sent Peter and John to prepare a Passover meal. When they asked him where to make the preparations, Jesus gave precise instructions. They were to look for a man carrying a jar of water, follow him into a house, ask the homeowner for directions to the guest room, and make preparations there. They followed Jesus' instructions and prepared the meal (Luke 22:7-13).

In the next scene, the hour came and Jesus took his place at the table along with the apostles. Luke tells us that Jesus said to them, "I have eagerly desired to eat this Passover with you before I suffer; for I tell you, I will not eat it until it is fulfilled in the kingdom of God" (22:15-16). With that, Jesus took a cup, gave thanks, and said, "Take this and divide it among yourselves; for I tell you that from now on I will not drink of the fruit of the vine until the kingdom of God comes" (22:17-18). Then Jesus took a loaf of bread, gave thanks, broke it, gave it to them, and said, "This is my body, which is given for you. Do this in remembrance of me" (22:19). After the supper, in the tradition of a Passover meal, Jesus took another cup and said, "This cup that is poured out for you is the new covenant in my blood" (22:20). As supper closed, Jesus told his apostles that one of them at the table would betray him. Although the bitter end was apparently determined, the one who betrayed him would still suffer woe. The disciples all wondered who would do this thing. But the conversation merged quickly into a dispute about who among them was the greatest. The disciples moved from worrying about betrayal to hoping for glory. Jesus responded promptly, reminding them that "the greatest among you must become like the youngest, and the leader like one who serves" (22:26). Jesus reminded them that he was one who served, and he reassured them that they would one day eat and drink at his Table in the Kingdom and that they would sit on thrones of judgment.

The world in which this supper took place was a broken world, no less than the world in which Antonia and I were trying to find our way when we first met, and no less than worlds where warring countries are trying to find their way at this very moment. The foretelling of destruction for the Temple and Jerusalem was uttered in a world where these were indeed threatened and eventually destroyed by political and social powers. In fact, the Temple had likely been destroyed already at the time that Luke was writing his Gospel. Not only was the world broken, but evil was a reality, and the people were conscious of God's judgment and cosmic danger no less than the people who had recited Noah's story again and again. This was a time of alertness, fear, and hope for God's intervention.

Alongside the brokenness of the world, several hopes were in the air that the early Christian community was breathing as they heard and told Luke's stories of Jesus. One hope was that the events of destruction and madness were signs of God's future breaking into the present, as it had been in times past. Another hope was that God's promised kingdom would indeed come, and was in fact near. Another hope was for a place of glory in the kingdom. And finally, the people expressed a hope for continuity between Jesus and themselves, as the words of Jesus' last supper with his disciples became words of institution in the Christian service of Communion (Eucharist). In relation to this last hope, early

Christian communities apparently used this text to guide their worship, and the final form of Luke's text may have been influenced by this usage. Some other ancient texts do not actually include the words of institution in 22:19-20, or they include only part of them. Luke' Gospel apparently provided a link for early Christians between Jesus' life, death, and resurrection and their own worship. This link gave hope.

The story of Jesus' last supper not only entered into a hoping world, but the story itself promised restoration. It promised to restore confidence in a world of fear and destruction, comfort in a threatening world, and guidance in a confusing world. Luke goes out of his way to help his readers see how broken the world is and how much people need signposts for restoration. The story, then, offers signposts, not by removing fear but by promising confidence, comfort, and guidance.

The story restores confidence (shared faith) by revealing Jesus at the Covenant Table with his disciples. The very act of breaking bread together sealed their covenant relationship; they were offering trust to one another, binding themselves together forever. For predictions of betrayal to follow so quickly after this covenant was devastating, but Jesus continued at the Table to promise that the disciples would eat and drink at his Table in the Kingdom. The promises would not destroy the realities ahead of them, but they would provide a way through and beyond those realities. This theme echoes the tension between optimism and pessimism discussed in Chapter One. God's promises were not to restore optimism; the situation was to get even worse, with the actual betrayal by Judas, denial by Peter, trial, and death. On the other hand, Jesus' last supper with his disciples would restore grounds for confidence; he invited a shared faith in God and God's future.

The story also restores comfort by assuring the disciples of God's presence with them. Within the Passover context of remembering God's deliverance of Israelites from slavery, the supper with Jesus communicated much: God's future was breaking into the present, God's kingdom was coming, they would have a place in the kingdom, and they could continue to celebrate covenant at Table with Jesus and one another. For early Christians, these comforts continued as they gathered to read the words of Luke and celebrate the Last Supper again and again in worship.

Finally, *this story restores guidance by giving explicit guidance to the disciples about how to act in this particular situation and how to act as they continue in discipleship.* Guidance is always a critical part of people's relationship with God, as witnessed in the other stories of this chapter. In this story, Jesus guides the disciples in how to select a place and prepare for the Passover meal; he instructs them in eating and drinking at the Table; he instructs them to remember him; and he instructs them to be a people who serve. We can place these instructions alongside the earlier praise of Jesus for the widow who gave all that she had (Luke 21:1-4), and the later instruction for the disciples at the Mount of Olives to pray to avoid the "time of trial" (22:40, 46). Viewing the story in context, we see the Last Supper as a time when the disciples were guided into action, both for the immediate moment and for their future ministries. On this note of action, the chapter concludes with reflections on identity and ministry in covenantal relationships.

Conclusion

This chapter began with the reality of broken communities, seen also in biblical study. Brokenness is everywhere we turn, but brokenness is not the final word in a covenantal universe. What emerges in studies of this chapter is a gushing of grace at the most unexpected moments. The grace that emerged from meetings with Antonia was mediated through a bishop, a doctoral student, and Antonia herself. Grace abounds in the biblical stories as well—stories of creation; of Noah's people and all living creatures; of Abraham, Sarah, and Hagar; of Jesus and his disciples. In all of these stories God is shown as concerned for all creation, for righteous living, for protecting the earth, for people and their legacies, and for restoring broken covenants with hope for God's future.

What is also revealed in the biblical texts is hope for a better world. Abraham and Sarah wanted a better future from God, who had sent them on a long journey to the Promised Land. Hagar, the

Egyptian slave girl, also wanted a better future for both herself and her son, Ishmael. Such hope awakens people to the promise-making God; such hope focuses attention on restoration—building toward justice and well-being for God's creation. As long as people have hope, they will find themselves building arks, traveling with God, and gathering at Jesus' Supper Table. The problem, of course, is that they will often perpetrate injustice in the process, as Sarai and Abram did to Hagar; they will also disagree about what God is asking them to do. Even after Antonia and I became close friends, we had to find ways to discuss difficult issues, to communicate and interpret our different views, and to stand for our commitments. We both cared deeply about God's future and the possibility of restoration, but we saw these differently. We had to discuss our different views with honesty and integrity while also loving one another. The blessing was that love and respect actually made disagreement and negotiation more possible than ever before.

Several visions for identity and ministry emerge from these diverse texts, although none of the texts can be reduced to the brief interpretations offered in this chapter. *First, the texts point to a vision of identity that is both particular and universal.* Certainly, the Noah, Abraham, Sarah, and Hagar stories point in this direction. Similarly, Antonia and I, and everyone else who was involved in the case study, were challenged to identify ourselves fully within our own contexts and, at the same time, to broaden ourselves by identifying with people in quite different contexts. This vision suggests that although a particular United Methodist local church may ground its identity in a particular racial-ethnic or geographical location, it can still be conscious of a deep relationship with the larger United Methodist and ecumenical connection. This vision further suggests that points of view and theological perspectives may differ from community to community and within each community, but the people may still be deeply connected in love. The very tension between the particular and universal stirs theological and ethical questions and keeps people searching for the will of God in the midst of their diversity. Even while people struggle with controversy or seek to take a unified stand on an ethical issue, they can offer love as the binding sign of Christian community and human family.

A second vision is to participate in ministries that seek and respond to the promises of God. All of the stories of this chapter point to God's future and the vigor of God as a promise-maker. To seek God's promises and live by them is a great challenge. It allows for neither optimism nor pessimism, but demands hope; it demands covenantal living. Sometimes covenant calls for actions of a particular kind (building an ark or going to a new land); sometimes it calls for developing habits of living in relation to creation (caring for animals or practicing circumcision or living as people who serve). Sometimes it simply calls for remembering and being grateful (remembering God's promises with the rainbow and remembering Jesus' life and death in the celebration of Communion). At all times, covenant pushes beyond caring for "my" people, or even caring only for people. It challenges us to minister with, to, and for all of God's creation.

Resources for Meditation

The following prayer for peace is from Saint Francis, who lived in Assisi, Italy, from approximately 1182 to 1226. Founder of the Franciscan Order, Francis witnessed to a simple way of living with God. Pray the prayer aloud slowly. Then consider what the prayer says about God's covenant with broken communities. Pray the prayer again.

> Lord, make me an instrument of Thy peace. Where there is hatred, let me sow love; where there is injury, pardon; where there is doubt, faith; where there is despair, hope; where there is sadness, joy; where there is darkness, light.

> O Divine Master, grant that I may not so much seek to be consoled, as to console; not so much to be understood, as to understand; not so much to be loved, as to love. For it is in giving that we receive, it is in pardoning that we are pardoned, it is in dying that we are born again to eternal life.

From *Instrument of Thy Peace: Revised Edition,*
by Alan Paton (Walker and Company, 1984).

Covenant and Call

Questions for Reflection

Choose one of the stories of this chapter—the story of Antonia or one of the biblical stories. Read it through slowly and meditatively. In the case of the biblical stories, read them from the Bible. Return to the stories and reflect on them using the following questions:

- What is revealed in the story about brokenness?
- What is revealed about God's action and the movements of God's grace?
- What is revealed about God's calling for the particular people in this story?
- What appear to be God's underlying purposes in giving these specific expectations and requirements?
- How does God's call in this story translate into God's calling for people today?
- What other discoveries have you made that are important for thinking about the future of the church?
- What discoveries have you made for your local church, your denomination, or the diverse religious communities in your area?

Endnotes

1 See "Connexion and Koinonia: Wesley's Legacy and the Ecumenical Ideal," by Brian E. Beck, in *Rethinking Wesley's Theology for Contemporary Methodism*, edited by Randy L. Maddox (Kingswood Books/Abingdon Press, 1998); pages 129–141.

2 See *An Interpretation of Religion: Human Responses to the Transcendent*, by John Hick (The MacMillan Press, 1989), and *The Myth of Christian Uniqueness: Toward a Pluralistic Theology of Religions,* edited by John Hick and Paul F. Knitter (Orbis Books, 1987).

3 See *Theology of Hope: On the Ground and the Implications of a Christian Eschatology*, by Jürgen Moltmann, translated by James W. Leitch (Harper & Row, Publishers, 1967).

4 This theme has been well developed by Delores S. Williams, a womanist scholar who finds the story of Hagar particularly powerful for African American women. See *Sisters in the Wilderness: The Challenge of Womanist God-Talk* (Orbis Books, 1993).

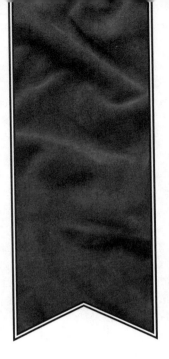

CHAPTER THREE

GOD'S CALL TO COVENANTAL COMMUNITIES

When I was a child, my local church in Baton Rouge, Louisiana, celebrated its 125th year. It was a grand celebration that lasted several days. The most memorable event was wearing nineteenth-century costumes to church on Sunday morning and entering a grand parade through the downtown area of the city. Some people rode in buggies pulled by horses; most of us walked. On the same day, we removed a box of historical papers from the cornerstone, and people shared from historical documents, events, and memories. A shift in consciousness took place in me during those days of celebration; I came to know the church as a historical reality.

Covenantal realities are not always so smooth and wonderful as celebrating the 125th anniversary of a local church, but they often inspire a sense of history. The purpose of this chapter is to explore covenantal communities in history—the creeds and diverse forms of historical communities and the covenantal convictions that have sustained them to follow their distinctive calls. The historical communities are introduced briefly, but a sampling of communities from different times and places gives a sense of the heritage out of which the future church will come. Particular attention is given to how the various communities have experienced grace, wrestled with problems and troubling questions, and lived God's call within their particular situations.

God's call to covenant communities can be filled with wonder, and also with fear and trepidation. This reality has already been evident in the stories of the previous chapter, and it becomes increasingly evident as we focus on God's call. Consider some of the realities that are uncovered in the biblical witness.

In Exodus 3:1-12, we find Moses calmly tending his father-in-law's sheep when a burning bush catches his eye. Looking at the bush, Moses hears a voice that tells him to remove his sandals because he is standing on holy ground. The voice calling from the bush identifies itself as "the God of your father" and the God of Abraham, Isaac, and Jacob. This great God of Moses' ancestors proceeds to tell Moses, "I have observed the misery of my people" (3:7). Then God declares the intent to deliver these people from their captors in Egypt. God asks Moses to go to Pharaoh and deliver the Israelites. Shocked, Moses asks "Why me?" God responds by promising to be with Moses, who will deliver the people and return to worship on the mountain where Moses is now standing.

In Luke 1:26-56, we meet another story of call. This time, a woman named Mary is approached by the angel Gabriel, who explains that Mary has found favor with God and will conceive a son, whom she is to name Jesus. The angel explains that her son "will be great, and will be called the Son of the Most High, . . . and will reign over the house of Jacob forever" (1:32-33). Mary asks how that can be since she is a virgin. The angel explains, "The power of the Most High will overshadow you." In response to the angel's explanations, Mary responds, "Here am I, the servant of the Lord; let it be with me according to your word" (1:38). Soon thereafter, Mary journeys to her relative Elizabeth, who has also conceived in a miraculous circumstance. At this point in Luke's story, Mary sings the Magnificat to Elizabeth:

My soul magnifies the Lord,
  and my spirit rejoices in God my Savior,
for he has looked with favor on the lowliness of his servant.
(Luke 1:47-48a)

In these two biblical stories, as in the story of my church's 125th anniversary celebration, remembrance and wonder are real. In all three, God is experienced in the moment and in history. Similarly, people are known as a community living through time. Moses is listening to the God of his ancestors, and Mary's story is told in relation to the historical house of David. We are told that Mary is engaged to Joseph, who is in David's line, and her son Jesus will inherit the throne of David. The biblical stories are far more explicit about God's call for the future than my shortened versions. Indeed, they are foundational stories in the lives of Jewish and Christian communities respectively. All three stories are turning points for the people involved, however; and this is the source of their power.

Although God does not call through every event in the same way, momentous events such as church anniversaries are often turning points for congregations. One congregation, in rediscovering their history as a mission church, was inspired to sponsor the formation of a new mission church as a way of celebrating their one hundredth year. This centennial church, convinced that it was dying, discovered new life as they remembered the past and found direction for a second century of ministry. Indeed, transformations take place in the unexpected experiences of remembrance and wonder, of God in the moment and God in history, of community life through time, of God's call for the future. With these possibilities in mind, we turn to history.

Covenantal Communities in History

In looking toward the past, we begin with historical statements regarding the church. First, it is important to note that the church was never one consolidated body, and never understood in one simple way. From the earliest days, as recorded in the New Testament, there were diverse forms of church, diverse political structures, diverse points of view, and diverse passions for mission. These variations sometimes led to schisms, sometimes to church councils to resolve differences (as the first-century Council of Jerusalem or the fourth-century Council of Nicaea); sometimes they were simply accepted as the different ways of neighboring communities.

Two words for church are central in the New Testament— *ekklesia* and *diakonia*. The former can be translated "called out and gathered community," and the latter "serving community." At the heart of the early church, then, were the central ideas that the church was called out, gathered, and sent forth to serve. Much more could be said of these definitions and understandings, but this brief glimpse does suggest that the distinctive qualities of covenantal communities were embodied in the earliest definitions of church. These accents continued, and they were elaborated and expressed in diverse ways as the church grew—both in the creeds and confessions of the church and in the living forms of church that emerged.

Covenant Expressed in Creeds

Creeds soon became a way for Christian churches to identify their central beliefs and values regarding God, the church, and Christian life. In the Apostles' Creed (traditional and ecumenical versions), the church was affirmed as "the holy catholic church." This definition was expanded in the Nicene Creed of A.D. 325 (as revised in A.D. 381 by the Council of Constantinople) to read "one holy catholic and apostolic Church."[1] Thus, the church was understood as *one* (a unified body), *holy* (of God), *apostolic* (carrying on God's work), and *catholic* (universal). Again, the basic qualities of covenant community were affirmed.

Other forms of expression became important during the Reformation, so the following affirmations were part of the Augsburg Confession (Lutheran):

> It is also taught among us that one holy Christian church will be and remain forever. This is the assembly of all believers among whom the Gospel is preached in its purity and the holy sacraments are administered according to the Gospel.[2]

Similar statements on preaching and the sacraments are found in many confessions and catechisms of Reformed churches.[3] There is also an emphasis on the priesthood of all believers in Lutheran and Reformed churches. At the same time, the accent on the "one holy catholic and apostolic church" persists in these creedal statements, with varied and expanded language.

Throughout this emerging history, most Christian churches continued to use the Nicene Creed alongside their later formulations. One reason the Nicene Creed has been so important in the contemporary ecumenical movement is that it represents church consensus before the first division into East and West. The Nicene-Constantinopolitan Creed is shared in a way that later creeds and confessions are not.

One further note is important regarding the creeds and confessions of various church bodies. Although many creeds included strong critiques of beliefs and practices that people rejected, the creeds often included a hint of humility as well. Consider, for example, the Presbyterians' Westminster Confession of Faith (1646) and the Church of England's Thirty-Nine Articles of Religion (1571):

> The purest churches under heaven are subject both to mixture and error; and some have so degenerated as to become no churches of Christ.[4]

> As the Church of Jerusalem, Alexandria, and Antioch, have erred; so also the Church of Rome hath erred, not only in their living and manner of Ceremonies, but also in matters of Faith.[5]

In these words, judgment is very obvious because the various churches were contending with one another in regard to truth and purity. At the same time, the statements do acknowledge the possibility of error, even in themselves.

Turning now to Methodist traditions, we note that John Wesley led his movement to carry a definition of church from the Articles of Religion of the Church of England:

> The visible church of Christ is a congregation of faithful men in which the pure Word of God is preached, and the Sacraments duly administered according to Christ's ordinance, in all those things that of necessity are requisite to the same.[6]

God's Call to Covenantal Communities

Note some of the features of this description. It is named first as *the church of Christ* and then as *a gathering of the faithful*. These opening words suggest a *koinonia* (sharing community) of the sort we discussed in Chapter Two, a view of church that is central in contemporary ecumenical discussions. In the earlier chapter, a link was made between the spirit of *koinonia* and what was embodied in the connection of early Methodism. The Articles of Religion also accent two other features of the church: *where the Word of God is preached,* and *the sacraments duly administered according to Christ's ordinance.* We see here the early Protestant accents on Word and sacrament, which are embodied in the words and deeds of the church and bound by the Word of God and Christ's ordinance. These descriptions of church also emphasize God's initiative and instructions, consistent with biblical studies of the previous chapter. All of these features are woven into the very definition of church.

Consider also "The Confession of Faith of the Evangelical United Brethren Church." This church and the former Methodist Church formed The United Methodist Church in 1968. In the E.U.B. Confession, several affirmations of the ecumenical church through the ages are carried forth:

> We believe the Christian Church is the community of all true believers under the Lordship of Christ. We believe it is one, holy, apostolic, and catholic. It is the redemptive fellowship in which the Word of God is preached by men divinely called, and the sacraments are duly administered according to Christ's own appointment. Under the discipline of the Holy Spirit the Church exists for the maintenance of worship, the edification of believers and the redemption of the world.[7]

Note that the first two accents of this confession are the same as those in the Methodist and Church of England Articles, namely the community of believers and the church's relationship to Christ. The next accents affirm the classical Nicene definition of church. As in the Methodist Article, the E.U.B. Confession reflects covenantal themes from previous chapters of this book, especially unity among the covenant people, the centrality of God and the ways of God, responsibilities expected of God's people, and the universality of the church. The E.U.B. Confession also carries the accent on Word and sacrament, which is amplified in relation to the church's role in worship, edification, and redemption of the world. The Confession thus carries themes from biblical and creedal traditions, as well as from the Protestant Reformation.

This brief historical review is neither comprehensive nor final. If you study the various definitions carefully, you will note different accents and wordings, the result of definitions that are shaped not only by history but also by the needs of the church and world at a particular time and place. Leonardo Boff highlights how different theological tendencies emerge at different times: "Each theological tendency has a truth to propose and corresponding errors to counter."[8] Further, each theological tendency serves the church in particular ways in a particular time and place; these often change over time. Boff says, "Because of this *diakonia* (service) that every true theology must offer the Church, no single theological tendency is enough."[9] This suggests that no theology is complete in itself, but every theology has responsibility to serve the church and world; its value might be measured by how well it serves. These ideas lead to questions about concrete forms and actions of covenant communities.

Covenant Expressed in Many Forms

As we enter explorations of covenantal communities, we now explore how Christian communities of the past and present have carried on historical traditions and also offered *diakonia* (service) in their distinctive contexts. We further explore how they have embodied and confounded covenantal relationships, and how God's work is revealed through these communities, even with their limitations. Drawing from these historical forms, we will draw implications and guidance for the future.

Households and House Churches

In Chapter Two we mentioned briefly Antonia's house church in Hungary. Her church stands in a long line of house churches throughout Christian history. Such churches meet in people's homes and provide a setting for small community gatherings and common work, contributing to the spiritual depth of members and the good of the larger community. During the Communist occupation of Central Europe, house churches also provided some added measure of freedom. Two practices among early Christian communities point in a similar direction, stirring visions for the future. These are ministries with households and house churches.

As for households, the first-century social structures were quite different from the structures in most of the modern world. Fathers in that earlier Mediterranean world could make major decisions for their entire household (extended family, workers, and workers' families). Thus, one person could be converted to Christianity and the entire household would follow. We find records of this practice in Acts and in Paul's letters. Cornelius is identified as "a devout man who feared God with all his household," giving alms generously and praying constantly (Acts 10:2; see also 10:24-33). Crispus, a synagogue leader, becomes "a believer in the Lord, together with all his household" (18:8).[10] We are told that one woman, Lydia, is also baptized with her household. She immediately offers the hospitality of her home to Paul and his companions (16:14-15). Stephanas, a member of the Corinthian congregation, is baptized with his household; in fact, they are among the few people baptized by Paul in Corinth (1 Corinthians 1:16). We are told in Paul's letters that Stephanas and his household were the first converts in Achaia (the Roman province where Corinth was located), and that they "devoted themselves to the service of the saints" (16:15). Paul also encourages the people to support Stephanas's work, and he describes his gratitude to Stephanas for refreshing his spirit and the spirit of the people in Corinth (16:16-18). In sum, these households provided some of the backbone of Paul's ministry.

Similar praise can be given to house churches. The house churches of different regions were important centers of ministry, and Paul also connected them with one another. In fact, the Corinthian church was probably divided into smaller groups that met in different parts of the large, diversified city and came together for worship and the Lord's Supper, a gathering that was sometimes abused (1 Corinthians 11:17-22; 14:26-33a). Paul also sent greetings from house churches and families to other Christians, as in the case of Aquila and Prisca (16:19). Aquila and Prisca (Priscilla) were Jewish Christians who had to evacuate from Rome under persecution from the government. Paul stayed with them in their home in Corinth and worked with them in their common trade of tent-making (Acts 18:1-3). He also wrote for the Romans to greet them and the church in their house; and he lavishly commended their work, for they "risked their necks for my life" (Romans 16:3-5).

The New Testament letters actually include many such greetings to individuals and the churches in their houses (Colossians 4:15; 2 Timothy 4:19; Philemon 1:1-2). The house churches were known for their spirit of hospitality and kinship, often providing alternative community for people whose own families and households were not intact.

Turning now to visions for the future church, households and house churches offer much promise; they can be formed as small congregations or as small communities within a larger congregation. Such groupings can provide a way to embody the idealistic description of the early church in Acts 2:42-47—studying, enjoying fellowship, breaking bread from house to house, praying, worshiping, participating in acts of wonder, and sharing possessions for the good of all. The full sharing described in Acts is often most possible for communities that are sufficiently small to live in close communion. The house churches can also provide opportunities for kinship among Christian peoples whose own family patterns are destructive or destroyed. At the same time, these groupings can be a source for critical reflection on Christian life (as Paul encouraged in 1 Corinthians 11:17-22; 14:26-33a), and they can be linked together and encouraged to care for the larger community.

Such activities can already be found in some parts of the contemporary church. Consider Korean and Korean-American churches, for example. These communities often emphasize ministries in families and small classes. They encourage families to worship together every day and find ways to serve others as a family. They also divide their larger congregations into small classes, which can meet weekly to share, pray, and care for one another. A somewhat different form of this ministry is found in one Native American church, which sponsors "Circles of Life" throughout southern California, led by "gatherers." The purpose of these groups is also to share, pray, and care for one another. The practice is intended to draw upon the traditional tribal organization of Native peoples, as well as the gathering traditions of peoples who first inhabited the southwest United States. The practice is also intended to extend the ministry of the larger congregation and serve the needs of Native people in the region.

Drawing from these contemporary practices and from the households and house churches of Paul's letters, we can project two possibilities for the contemporary church: the encouragement of religious practice in families, and the encouragement of house churches or small and regular gatherings of covenant communities. Certainly these ministries would include worship and prayer, practical sharing, breaking bread together, active service in the larger church or community, study, fellowship, and acts of hospitality to others. The possibilities are endless!

Monastic Communities

Monastic life emerged very early in Christian history. From the third century onward, hermits lived by themselves or monks lived in community. The purpose was to live in a sanctified way, usually concentrating on prayer and work. The desert fathers and mothers of Egypt were among the first to live such a life, but monasticism became a major way of Christian life in the British Isles as well, since the social organization of the Celtic people was largely centered around clans with local chiefs. The early Christian monasteries were similarly formed in small communities with abbots for leaders, which was a natural form of life for the people. The Celts (largely from Ireland, Scotland, and Wales) were also great pilgrims, and they carried their monastic traditions with them as they moved across Europe.

The Benedictines also had broad influence on monastic formation. St. Benedict, born in Southern Italy around 480, initially lived as a hermit himself; but a community formed around him. Later he actively formed monasteries and formulated the Benedictine Rule, which still guides Benedictine and other religious communities. Many other religious orders have also been formed, including the Franciscans, the Poor Clares, the Dominicans, and the Taizé Community (ecumenical). Each community has its distinctive charisms (gifts) and purposes.

Monastic life is an ever-present possibility, not only for people who join religious orders and enter monasteries but also for those who participate regularly or occasionally in these communities or in their disciplines. People sometimes go on personal or group retreats to monastic houses, and they sometimes align themselves with a particular monastery and follow the disciplines of that community while living in their homes and carrying on their normal work and play.

My colleague Frank Rogers and I developed a course that was designed to emulate some dimensions of monastic life. The course, Communal Learning and Care of the Earth, was part of the seminary curriculum; but it was taught in an unusual way. The class sessions were extended to include times for worship, work (physical labor in projects selected and designed by the class), study, and a common meal. The course, by its very design, stirred closeness among participants, established a shared rhythm of work and worship, and motivated us to discern needs in the community that we might address in our common work. Among other things, these classes sponsored a renovation of the children's playground and a major landscaping project, which eventually became a biblical-meditation garden with draught-tolerant, indigenous plants that are named in the Bible. These projects led to others.

Drawing from historic monastic communities and these contemporary practices, we can imagine much for the future church. Congregations, church boards and committees, ministry teams, and specially organized groups might enter covenant to live in monastic rhythms, for example. To do so would mean practicing disciplines of worship and prayer, work, study, and group organization, following daily or weekly rhythms. It might also include retreats and other times set aside for silence or intense living together in the rhythms of community life.

Parish Churches and Class Meetings

One last pair of historical forms is considered here for the church. One is the parish church, based in a geographical area to which and for which the church bears responsibility. The other is the class meeting, which emerged in seventeenth-century Lutheranism and grew into a lively movement within the Wesleyan connection. These two church forms are considered together because they are complementary and because they provided a broad system of ministry in the early days of the Wesleyan movement.

The parish system emerged naturally from European feudal systems in which every geographical area had a feudal lord and provisions for religious life. The intention of the parish church was originally to tend to the religious life of people in that area, and it emerged into the religious tending of all life in that area. The parish structure involved the church in public ministry—tending to the well-being of the people, land, and social structures within the parish. In many countries and through much of history, the parish church was interwoven with the civil government. This was not the case in the United States, where religion and state were separated by constitutional authority. But even in the United States, the parish structure of Catholic and Episcopal churches encouraged religious institutions to take responsibility for public care, including education, health, and issues of local concern. In some countries, the parish structure has also encouraged ecumenical work. In England and New Zealand, for example, ecumenical parishes flourish in some areas. In these, Anglican, Methodist, and Reformed churches sponsor one parish church together.

Class meetings originally emerged alongside a parish system. Classes were small groups that met to pray, study Scripture, and reflect on their lives. Variously named, these small groups were originally part of a pietistic revival in Germany in the seventeenth century, encouraging people to gather weekly and support one another in their spiritual lives. The practice spread, and in eighteenth-century England, similar groups were formed in some Puritan and Anglican communities. John Wesley and early leaders of the Methodist movement began a similar practice to raise money for building a church in Bristol. They asked people to bring a penny a week to their small band (class) meetings, and while they were gathered each week, they prayed, sang, studied Scripture, and reflected on how they lived their lives. The classes were designed to nurture the spiritual and ethical life of group members.[11] In the modern church, class meetings are still practiced actively by Korean and Korean-American churches in the Methodist tradition. Also, the base communities of Latin American churches bear close resemblance, including prayer, Bible study, and reflection on life practices.

Considering parish churches and class meetings together is somewhat unusual, but the combination reflects the genius of the early Methodist movement in Britain. It is not surprising that John and Charles Wesley did not want to separate from the Church of England. They were both connectionally oriented, and they trusted in parish life as a source of lively faith. Their hope in the evangelical revival was to enliven faith, not to replace the faith structures that were already in place. They sought to complement the ministry of the parish church by providing preaching services, societies (groups of thirty to forty) for the edification of people in the parish, and bands and classes (groups of four to twelve) for spiritual support and challenge. They still expected their people to participate in regular worship and Eucharist within their parishes and to continue working in parish ministries.

Drawing from the traditions and contemporary forms of parish churches and class meetings, we can find many challenges for the future church. One is to establish structures and programs to tend to the public life of a neighborhood, city, town, or region. Another is to establish structures and programs to tend to the spiritual nurture of people within the Christian community, particularly in the form of small groups that involve people in praying and studying together, and in reflecting and making commitments for their daily lives.

Covenantal Convictions

In the Introduction we discussed some of the convictions about God that undergirded Jewish and Christian communities of the past. Now we return to those convictions, giving particular attention to the significance of the church's living by grace (sacramental living) and living in relationship (trinitarian living). Convictions about God's grace and God's triune being did not arise as abstractions or as rules to be followed and requirements for belief. They arose in historical communities for which they were important for reasons imbedded in daily living. They continued because they offered vitality to later communities as well, giving inspiration and guidance and evoking questions and wonder. They have been passed on, contested, revised, and reaffirmed over time. This does not make them rules or beliefs for us today. We need to continue the tradition of passing on, contesting, revising, and reaffirming as we are moved by the living Spirit of God.

Living by Grace—Sacramental Living

At the heart of Wesleyan theology is God's grace and the power of that grace to transform human lives. These principles stand at the heart of Charles Wesley's hymns and John Wesley's theology. Grace is understood as a free gift of God, which evokes a human response and requires human responsibility. Thus, recent descriptions of John Wesley's theology are titled *Responsible Grace, Grace and Responsibility,* and *The Limits of "Love Divine."*[12] In all of these works, the fullness of God's grace is expressed with hope for human response. God's grace is also understood as pointing to God's future, as evidenced by the title of another recent book on John Wesley's theology, *The New Creation.*[13] For Wesley, the future hope included new birth for human lives and the renewal of all creation.[14] These themes are familiar echoes of the covenantal themes identified in the Introduction—initiated by God, binding communities, calling people to action, pointing to future.

This discussion of living by grace is here titled "Sacramental Living" because it centers on receiving and sharing the blessings of God. More precisely, it centers on receiving and mediating God's grace for the sanctification of human life and the well-being of the world. The sacraments themselves, central to Wesley's understanding of church, are ways by which we participate in God's grace as a Christian community. Participating in the sacraments also heightens our awareness of God's grace in many corners of our lives. Not only did Wesley encourage frequent observance of Eucharist, but he also encouraged his people to participate in the multiple means of grace, or the multiple ways by which God's grace is mediated.

The sacraments are understood in Christianity as covenantal acts. John Wesley carried on this emphasis, using covenantal language throughout his discussions of baptism and Eucharist. Wesley understood baptism as initiation into God's covenant, cleansing of sins, admission into the body of Christ, and regeneration (new birth) as children of God and heirs of God's kingdom.[15] For Wesley, infant baptism was appropriate because God, through divine grace, is the primary actor in the sacrament. Baptism ideally leads to a life of repentance, faith, and obedience—the fruits of God's ongoing work in human lives. This understanding of baptism leads naturally to Eucharist, a covenantal act that renews us continually. Wesley urged people to "constant communion," saying, "It is the duty of every Christian to receive the Lord's Supper as often as he can."[16] Wesley understood Eucharist as a remembrance of Christ's self-giving in life and death, a means of forgiveness and pardon from past sins, renewal of our souls and bodies to follow God, a promise of glory,

84

and potentially a converting sacrament (conferring grace even though undeserved).[17] Eucharist, like baptism, is a covenantal act that conveys God's grace and strengthens people to live by that grace.

Unlike the sacraments, which are attributed to origins in Jesus' ministry, the means of grace are a broad list that Wesley named differently in different contexts. They include the sacraments, as well as other acts of grace-seeking and grace-sharing. One list includes prayer, searching the Scriptures, and receiving the Lord's Supper.[18] Another list includes church attendance, communicating, fasting, private prayer, and reading Scripture, as well as an emphasis on doing temporal and spiritual good in every way one can.[19] Wesley claimed that these means of grace are ordained by God and contribute to renewing people's souls.[20]

In light of this discussion, one can identify God's grace at work in the church's ongoing life. In that spirit, Leonardo Boff (Roman Catholic) identifies the church as the sacrament of the Holy Spirit,[21] and Jürgen Moltmann (Lutheran) describes the church as living in the presence and power of the Holy Spirit.[22] For both, the church is the way by which God's grace continues to work in the world. God's grace is a sacramental presence. As we turn now to God's call for the future church, we might identify three particular ways in which the sacramental grace of God is expressed—as a relationship, as a way of living, and as a source of growing in faith toward God's future.

Grace as a Relationship

Grace is God's primary way of being in relationship with creation. Grace is visible in God's movements—creating, redeeming, and sustaining the world. For human beings, grace is an invitation to be restored by God to the image of God; it is an invitation to be fully blessed by God's unsurpassable love and to participate fully in God's works of love. Thus, the relationship of grace is one that involves receiving and giving.

The reason John Wesley and followers in Wesleyan traditions have looked to multiple sources for God's revelation is God's relationship with every aspect of creation. To say that God is revealed through Scripture, tradition, experience, and reason is to say that God is revealed everywhere; wherever we turn, God's grace is available to touch and transform us. Excellent discussions are available regarding Wesley's intentions and methods in drawing upon these four sources, but the purpose here is more simple. The purpose here is to uncover Wesley's passion for relating with God in every situation and through every source available. This passion for relationship with God is also our calling.

Grace as a Way of Living

Much has been said already about Wesley's emphasis on grace as a way of living. In Wesley's preaching and writing, God's grace and human response are always in the foreground. When Wesley writes about the church, he does not conclude with doctrines but with encouragement for people to walk with God. He urges people to "walk worthy of the vocation wherewith we are called," which means "to think, speak, and act in every instance, in a manner worthy of our Christian calling." [23] In short, the measure of the church is not doctrinal consensus but how people live.

These words do not mean that doctrine is unimportant to Wesley; he enters doctrinal discussions and advocacy with passion. He would probably be enthusiastic about William Abraham's encouragement of the modern church to engage in doctrinal conversation and reflect on doctrinal essentials.[24] At the same time, John and Charles Wesley focused their ministries on proclaiming the transformative power of God's grace. Efforts to identify parameters of doctrine were always in service of that larger purpose. Certainly John Wesley's writing on the church concludes with the focus of walking with God. Doctrine is not an end in itself; it is a way to express God and nurture Christian discipleship, which includes believing and all other forms of Christian action.

The emphasis on a way of living is nowhere more evident than in Wesley's discussion of why constant communion is so important. He says of the eucharist:

> This is the food of our souls: This gives strength to perform
> our duty, and leads us on to perfection. If, therefore, we have
> any regard for the plain command of Christ, if we desire the

pardon of our sins, if we wish for strength to believe, to love and obey God, then we should neglect no opportunity of receiving the Lord's Supper.[25]

Note that the emphasis here is not on the well-being of the individual in isolation, nor on the salvation of disembodied souls. The emphasis is on believing, loving, and obeying God. The emphasis is on living by grace.

Grace as a Source of Growing in Faith Toward God's Future

In light of what has been said, the implication is clear. Drawing from Christian tradition and Wesleyan theology, people can trust in God's grace to support and guide them as they look toward God's future. The class meetings discussed earlier in this chapter reveal much about the desire of early Methodist leaders to support and guide people in daily living and in their continuing formation and transformation as followers of Christ. The assumption was not that people would grow better and better, but that God would continue to work miracles in their lives. The hope, then, was to challenge and encourage people in holiness of heart and life. Classes offered mentoring by a small community. At the same time, the means of grace offered ways to nourish faith. Both contributed to the ability of people to live by grace and grow in grace.

Living in Relationship—Trinitarian Living

Unlike grace, many people view the Trinity as an obscure doctrine. They have difficulty discerning why this belief was ever important to early communities and what possible vibrancy it can yield today. At the same time, the Trinity has been a central Christian conviction, anchoring covenantal communities of the past and present. For this reason, we turn now to the Trinity—a conviction about God that is vitally important for the future church. Here we see glimpses of the powerful relationships within God, which mysteriously embrace the diversity and unity of God. Here we discover why recent theologians are so excited by the Trinity. Note that the themes parallel those of the previous section on grace.

Trinity as a Relationship

In the Introduction we discussed the heart of Trinity as relational: pointing to relationships within God, which offer visions for human relations with God and creation. This idea is more natural to some cultures than to others. Korean theologian Jung Young Lee draws on East Asian traditions (China, Japan, and Korea) to describe trinitarian thinking.[26] His description echoes and expands themes of this book. For example, he explains that trinitarian thinking focuses people on relationships within God—the "and" and "between" in the Father-Son relationship. It also focuses on relationships between God and the world—the way in which Jesus was in the world but not of the world (John 17:6-16). Such thinking suggests possibilities for trinitarian living as well—living that is marked by full, inclusive, loving, and respectful relationships.

Three practical examples from Lee suggest how Christian people might encourage more full trinitarian relationships in their daily life together. In church life, trinitarian worship would focus not only on the God-human relationship but also on the cosmos. People would be directed to heaven and earth (the whole earth) and also to the relation between them. In family life, people would focus on their relationships of love with one another and with God. And in the larger world, trinitarian relationships would encourage people to be inclusive and respectful of others. Lee sees parallels between the coequality of the three in the Trinity and the coequality of various ethnic and racial groups in society. Full and respectful living with others reflects trinitarian relationships.

Trinity as a Way of Living

The focus on trinitarian relationships leads naturally to trinitarian living. What is this way of living? What patterns of community life are needed? What kind of Christian responsibility is required in the larger society? Answers to these questions emerge from many parts of the world.

Trinitarian living is, first of all, communal. The Brazilian theologian Leonardo Boff describes the Trinity as a vision for human communities:

> The community of Father, Son and Holy Spirit becomes the
> prototype of the human community dreamed of by those who

wish to improve society and build it in such a way as to make it into the image and likeness of the Trinity.[27]

These words lay out a bold demand, calling people to be builders—to build communities that reflect the triune God and to build a society in the likeness of God.

Trinitarian living also requires people to be involved in earthy realities. Josiah Young argues that the Trinity is a very earthy doctrine and that John Wesley's trinitarian faith was at the heart of his opposition to slavery. From Young's perspective, Wesley had a view of Jesus as fully human and fully divine, and a view of the Trinity as fully one and fully three. He argues that when people are committed to the earthiness of Jesus and the Trinity as fully grounded in the earth, they are not able to oppress others by taboos or racial and economic distancing. This very commitment is what Young sees as the heart of John Wesley's critique of slavery in his time, for slavery reveals the failure of love and the emergence of inhumanity.[28]

Trinitarian living is, thus, guided by love. Young argues that trinitarian faith is measured by our love for others. In particular he says that when people participate in economic and racial injustice or become "contemptuous of another so-called race," they are not worshiping the triune God or the God "incarnate in sinful flesh."[29] In short, true faith in the triune God, who is grounded in earth, will ground us in earth as well; it will inspire love and justice in our daily dealings. Malcolm Tan Thian Hock echoes a similar theme when he advocates a trinitarian faith that contributes to humanization. He recognizes that humanization is much needed in the Asian Pacific region where Western imperialism has continued to exert influence. In response he turns to the Trinity, which urges people to mutual love, care, and respect.[30]

These brief reflections do not answer all questions about trinitarian living, but they do suggest a vision that is communal, earthy, and loving.

Trinity as a Source of Growing in Faith Toward God's Future

The vision of the previous section is almost overwhelming, but the very richness of the Trinity offers much hope for Christian growth. Of course, we may ask, How do people grow when faced with the multi-faceted work of God and the diversity of the church? In this last section, the triune God is seen as an inspiration, support, and pattern for growing in faith as we look toward God's future.

Sondra Matthaei borrows a phrase from Charles Wesley, calling people to be "transcripts of the Trinity."[31] She describes the Wesleyan view of Trinity as "a pattern for Christian life"—a pattern that inspires "communion with the Three-One God and our neighbors."[32] Specifically she argues that Wesley understood the way of salvation as *"growing in communion* with God and neighbor"[33] (accent hers). She draws upon John Wesley's sermon on the Beatitudes to develop this central idea, describing how Jesus offered an "invitation to communion," "deepening of communion," and "full communion."[34]

These offerings of Jesus involve people on a journey that is difficult but always promising; it also raises questions for the church's ministry. What actions are needed to invite people into communion, to deepen their communion, and to move them toward fuller communion? In simple language, how can we encourage people into fuller love of God and neighbor? These questions set the stage for the next chapter, but hope already comes to us in the triune God, who offers communion again and again.

Conclusion

In light of the covenantal heritage discussed in this chapter, what is the mission of the church? That question forms the center of Chapter Four, yet this chapter already points some directions. Imagine the church as a group of folks traveling through a deep canyon with steep sides. We are like a wandering group of nomads; we seek the best way to go, even when we can only see a few yards in front of ourselves. Even with the difficulties, however, we carry a rich heritage, which provides maps, tools, and compass. The heritage is also alive; thus, it echoes through the canyon walls, reminding us that God has called covenantal communities in the past, and God calls us still.

The church has understood and formed itself in many different ways through Christian history, and no one pattern will ever embody the whole of God's call. Such a realization evokes humility about any particular belief or practice; it also stirs excitement about what might yet unfold as people seek God's guidance in the present day. The anchors of the past, and the visions of God's grace and God's triune nature, provide markers. People still seek God's unique call for the future church.

Resources for Meditation

Return to the creeds and confessions quoted in this chapter. Choose one that is particularly meaningful to you. Read it slowly and meditatively, lingering over each word. As you are led in your silent meditation, pray for the church, both as it is and as it could be.

Choose from the following hymns or litanies (as found in *The United Methodist Hymnal*) to sing or read with your community:

"Many Gifts, One Spirit" (114)
"The Church's One Foundation" (545 or 546)
"O Church of God, United" (547)
"In Christ There Is No East or West" (548)
"Forward Through the Ages" (555)
"Litany for Christian Unity" (556)
"We Are the Church" (558)
"Christ Is Made the Sure Foundation" (559)
"For the Unity of Christ's Body" (564)
"One Bread, One Body" (620)

Questions for Reflection

- If your study group were asked to write a creed or confession, what would you include about the church? Why?
- Choose one of the covenantal forms discussed in this chapter (households and house churches, monastic communities, parish churches, or class meetings). Reflect on what draws you to that form and what practical possibilities it holds for your local church or church body (council, committee, board, district, or annual conference).
- What convictions about grace and Trinity are most suggestive to you about the future mission of your own congregation?

God's Call to Covenantal Communities   91

Endnotes

1 See *The United Methodist Hymnal* (The United Methodist Publishing House, 1989); pages 880–882.

2 From "The Augsburg Confession, Articles of Faith and Doctrine, VII. [The Church]" (1530); in *Creeds of the Churches: A Reader in Christian Doctrine From the Bible to the Present*, Third Edition, edited by John H. Leith (John Knox Press, 1982); page 70. The accent on preaching and the sacraments is elaborated in the remainder of the Article.

3 See "Reformed Creeds," in *Creeds of the Churches: A Reader in Christian Doctrine From the Bible to the Present*, Third Edition, edited by John H. Leith (John Knox Press, 1982); pages 127–230.

4 From "The Westminster Confession of Faith" (1646), in *Creeds of the Churches: A Reader in Christian Doctrine From the Bible to the Present*, Third Edition, edited by John H. Leith (John Knox Press, 1982); page 222.

5 From "The Thirty-Nine Articles of Religion, XIX. Of the Church" (American Revision of 1801), in *Creeds of the Churches: A Reader in Christian Doctrine From the Bible to the Present*, Third Edition, edited by John H. Leith (John Knox Press, 1982); page 273.

6 From "The Articles of Religion of The Methodist Church, Article XIII—Of the Church," in *The Book of Discipline of The United Methodist Church—1996.* Copyright © 1996 by The United Methodist Publishing House; page 60. Used by permission. John Wesley confirmed the significance of this article again in his later life when the danger of schism was rising between the Methodist movement and the Church of England. See particularly Sermon 74, "Of the Church," by John Wesley. In this sermon, Wesley also affirmed many traditional understandings of the church (as discussed in this chapter) and their import for ecumenical relations and ethical living.

7 From "The Confession of Faith of The Evangelical United Brethren Church, Article V—The Church," in *The Book of Discipline of The United Methodist Church—1996.* Copyright © 1996 by The United Methodist Publishing House; page 65. Used by permission.

8 From *Church: Charism and Power: Liberation Theology and the Institutional Church,* by Leonardo Boff, translated by John W. Diercksmeier (SCM Press, Inc., 1985); page 13.

9 From *Church: Charism and Power: Liberation Theology and the Institutional Church,* by Leonardo Boff, translated by John W. Diercksmeier (SCM Press, Inc., 1985); page 13.

10 See other examples of conversions, baptisms, and ministries with entire households in Acts 11:1-18 and 16:25-34. Note, also, that Paul often greets families and not simply individuals as he writes distant churches, for example in Romans 16:3-16.

11 A fuller description of the class meetings can be found in *Accountable Discipleship: Living in God's Household*, by Steven W. Manskar (Discipleship Resources, 2000).

12 *Responsible Grace: John Wesley's Practical Theology*, by Randy L. Maddox (Kingswood Books, 1994). *Grace and Responsibility: A Wesleyan Theology for Today*, by John B. Cobb, Jr. (Abingdon Press, 1995). *The Limits of "Love Divine": John Wesley's Response to Antinomianism and Enthusiasm*, by W. Stephen Gunter (Kingswood Books, 1989).

13 *The New Creation: John Wesley's Theology Today*, by Theodore Runyon (Abingdon Press, 1998).

14 See, for example, the following sermons by John Wesley: Sermon 18, "The Marks of the New Birth"; Sermon 45, "The New Birth"; Sermon 4, "Scriptural Christianity"; Sermon 26, "Upon Our Lord's Sermon on the Mount, Discourse VI"; Sermon 63, "The General Spread of the Gospel."

15 See "A Treatise on Baptism," by John Wesley.

16 From Sermon 101, "The Duty of Constant Communion," by John Wesley.

17 See Sermon 101, "The Duty of Constant Communion," by John Wesley.

18 See Sermon 16, "The Means of Grace," by John Wesley.

19 See "Journal from November 1, 1739, to September 3, 1741," journal entry on December 31, 1739, by John Wesley.

20 See Sermon 16, "The Means of Grace," by John Wesley.

21 See *Church: Charism and Power: Liberation Theology and the Institutional Church*, by Leonardo Boff, translated by John W. Diercksmeier (SCM Press, Inc., 1985); pages 144–153.

22 See *The Church in the Power of the Spirit: A Contribution to Messianic Ecclesiology*, by Jürgen Moltmann, translated by Margaret Kohl (Harper & Row, Publishers, 1977); pages 198–207.

23 From Sermon 74, "Of the Church," by John Wesley, which quotes Ephesians 4:1.

24 See *Waking from Doctrinal Amnesia: The Healing of Doctrine in The United Methodist Church*, by William J. Abraham (Abingdon Press, 1995); pages 56–65. See also "Discerning Unity in Essentials," by William J. Abraham, in *Unity, Liberty, and Charity: Building Bridges Under Icy Waters*,

edited by Donald E. Messer and William J. Abraham (Abingdon Press, 1996); pages 58–72.

25 From Sermon 101, "The Duty of Constant Communion," by John Wesley.

26 See *The Trinity in Asian Perspective,* by Jung Young Lee (Abingdon Press, 1996); pages 50–65, 180–219. Lee suggests that people would also engage interacting symbols of heaven, earth, and humanity. One particular example for Lee is the symbolization associated with baptism—heavens (heaven), water (earth), and descending dove (creature linking heaven and earth).

27 From *Trinity and Society,* by Leonardo Boff, translated by Paul Burns (Orbis Books, 1988); page 7.

28 See "Some Assumptions and Implications Regarding John Wesley's View of the Trinity: 'The Root of All Vital Religion,'" by Josiah Young, in *Quarterly Review,* Vol. 18, No. 2, Summer 1998; pages 140–147.

29 From "Some Assumptions and Implications Regarding John Wesley's View of the Trinity: 'The Root of All Vital Religion,'" by Josiah Young, in *Quarterly Review,* Vol. 18, No. 2, Summer 1998; page 147. Used by permission.

30 See "Evangelization Toward Trinitarian Inclusiveness in the Asia Pacific Area: A Wesleyan Perspective," by Malcolm Tan Thian Hock, in *Quarterly Review,* Vol. 18, No. 2, Summer 1998; pages 155–166. According to Hock, the Trinity also represents the communality that is important to Asian Pacific peoples; it points to the possibility of being and belonging at the same time.

31 Quoted in "Transcripts of the Trinity: Communion and Community in Formation for Holiness of Heart and Life," by Sondra Matthaei, in *Quarterly Review,* Vol. 18, No. 2, Summer 1998; page 123. Used by permission. The hymn quoted, by Charles Wesley, is #7 in *A Collection of Hymns for the Use of the People Called Methodists* (1780).

32 From "Transcripts of the Trinity: Communion and Community in Formation for Holiness of Heart and Life," by Sondra Matthaei, in *Quarterly Review,* Vol. 18, No. 2, Summer 1998; page 123. Used by permission.

33 From "Transcripts of the Trinity: Communion and Community in Formation for Holiness of Heart and Life," by Sondra Matthaei, in *Quarterly Review,* Vol. 18, No. 2, Summer 1998; page 124. Used by permission.

34 From "Transcripts of the Trinity: Communion and Community in Formation for Holiness of Heart and Life," by Sondra Matthaei, in *Quarterly Review,* Vol. 18, No. 2, Summer 1998; pages 123–135. Used by permission. See also Sermon 22, "Upon Our Lord's Sermon on the Mount, Discourse II," by John Wesley.

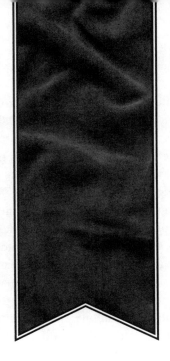

CHAPTER FOUR

CALLED TO GOD'S FUTURE

When someone in our family is out after dark, we always turn the light on to welcome the person home and to help him or her have a safe entry. This costs us some money in electricity and some effort to remember, but whenever one of us arrives home on a dark night, we know we are welcomed and loved.

This family tradition is sparked for me by the mystifying story in Matthew 25:1-13. The parable told by Matthew is found in the middle of several "kingdom of heaven" teachings of Jesus. In this parable, Jesus tells a story about ten bridesmaids who took their lamps and went to meet the bridegroom. Their responsibility as bridesmaids was to wait alongside the road for the bride and groom in order to greet them and escort them from one ceremony in the bride's house to the marriage feast in the home of the groom. In short, their responsibility was to welcome the new bride and groom into the household.

Notice that these bridesmaids did not have to perform any major feats or do anything that required great skill; they simply had to wait and keep their lanterns lighted so that they were available when the bride and groom arrived. As the story goes, five of the maidens—the foolish ones—took their lamps but did not take flasks of oil to refill the lamps. The other five maidens—the wise ones— took their lamps along with extra oil. Now, as life is unpredictable, the bridegroom was delayed and the maidens slept. But at midnight, someone saw the bridegroom coming and shouted. The maidens jumped to their feet and trimmed their lamps, but the foolish maidens were out of oil and out of light. The wise maidens did not have extra oil for the others, so the foolish ones had to go off and find oil in the middle of the night. In the meantime, the wise bridesmaids escorted the bride and groom to the wedding feast and went inside to join the welcoming, joyous event. When the foolish maidens returned, the lord of the house said that he did not know them. They were too late.

I have always thought of this as a harsh tale. The poor, foolish maidens were closed out of joy because they were not prepared. The text ends with this warning: "Keep awake therefore, for you know neither the day nor the hour" (Matthew 25:13). Matthew was actually writing this Gospel during harsh times. It was between the time when Jesus walked and talked on the earth and the time when Jesus would come again, as he had promised. The early Christians faced enormous difficulty as they tried to remain faithful, even in the midst of their disappointment that Jesus still had not come again as they expected. They also lived after the destruction of the Temple in Jerusalem, which was a devastating blow to the Jewish community. Matthew's community lived in a time when Jews were recreating their traditions to be less centered in the Temple and more centered in study houses, or synagogues, spread around the countryside. They lived in a time when Christians were creating their traditions in order to keep the Jesus stories alive and to live their lives according to the ways of God. These people asked a lot of questions, and Matthew responded to their questions by telling

them many Jesus stories about watching and waiting and being prepared for Jesus's second coming.

Consider this story. It is very complex, of course, but the
central message is quite simple. God's kingdom—the great feast—is
coming, but we do not know when. In short, the ways of God are
beyond our understanding. Thus, our job is quite simple; our job is to
keep the lights burning until the bridegroom—Jesus—arrives. That is
our mission: We can never know God fully, but our job is simply to
keep the lights burning so as to light the way and welcome God
whenever and wherever God appears. We are bridesmaids and light-
bearers, standing ready to light the way.

Herein lies the challenge for this concluding chapter: How
are we, in our covenantal and called communities, to live toward
God's future? This question turns us to mission—the mission of the
church and the mission of every Christian. The mission of the
bridesmaids was to be prepared, to light the way, to welcome and
travel as companions, and to celebrate with the bridal couple. What
kind of preparation, light, welcoming companionship, and celebration are we called to share as we, in this time and place, live
toward God's future?

Call to God's Future

We are faced with the mystery of future. We are faced with
eschatology and its reflections on last things—variously identified as
God's kingdom, kingdom of Heaven, God's new creation, or in
some recent theology, God's kin-dom. We are faced, also, with the
reality that some of these last things are already realized and some
are yet to come. All of them challenge us, however, to reflect upon
ourselves and reform the ways we live with God and God's creation. Such concerns were important to Matthew, whose own
idealistic visions of church were mixed with realistic images of a
flawed church and flawed Christian people.[1] The concerns are also
raised in apocalyptic writings, such as Daniel and Revelation, which
unveil mysteries (hidden truths) and point to the future. The concerns are raised with intensity yet again as we begin a new century;

they command the church's attention as we wonder what God wants of us now.

Nowhere is the spirit of God's future more vivid than in Jesus' first public act of ministry, as told by Luke (Luke 4:14-30). Arriving home in Nazareth, Jesus goes to the synagogue. When he stands to read the scroll, he says:

> The Spirit of the Lord is upon me,
> because he has anointed me
> to bring good news to the poor.
> He has sent me to proclaim release to the captives
> and recovery of sight to the blind,
> to let the oppressed go free,
> to proclaim the year of the Lord's favor.
>
> (Luke 4:18-19)

In this text, Jesus announces that the Spirit of God is upon him, and the Spirit has anointed him. He is not making a private claim but is recognizing that God has gifted and commissioned him. Further, Jesus recognizes his particular mission: to proclaim release for captives, sight for the blind, freedom for the oppressed, and Jubilee for everyone. His gifts are a commissioning to proclaim and act for God.

When people hear these things, they are amazed and impressed that Joseph's son has spoken with such power. Jesus, however, does not let well-enough alone. Instead of performing a miracle and enjoying the glory, he tells two challenging stories that remind people of earlier days when God performed miracles through ordinary people outside of Israel. He shifts attention away from himself to other people, like the widow of Zarephath, who provided food for Elijah during a severe famine. Jesus turns people's attention to bold action and challenging stories. After the stories Jesus is no longer welcome, and the people drive him out of town. For Jesus, to respond to God's future was to walk with God's Spirit, even into controversy, for the sake of fulfilling God's hopes for the world.

Although this story of Jesus seems quite distant from Jesus' story in Matthew of the wise and foolish maidens, it is actually similar in three critical ways. Whatever mission people are given, whether to light the way for a bride and groom or to proclaim release to the captives and let the oppressed go free, *a mission is a sacred trust from God, people are called to act, and their actions prepare the way for God's future.* Thus, we turn to these themes in the bridesmaids' story. In so doing, we face the challenging call of God's future.

Being Prepared

Being prepared is the most visible meaning in the bridesmaids' story. Being prepared begins with receiving and appreciating the gifts that God has given. It continues as we recognize the larger purpose of our gifts and use them as they were intended.[2] Being prepared further involves tending our gifts so that they are available when we most need them. In the story of the maidens, the most obvious gift was light. The most obvious purpose was to light the way for the newlyweds. To be prepared was to keep enough oil for the lamps so that they would last late into the night.

Drawing from this story, we recognize that being prepared has to do with receiving, appreciating, using, and tending the gifts we are given. This is a first dimension of mission, and it goes far beyond the popular connotations of being prepared in purely material terms. We are called to receive, appreciate, and use our gifts because they come from God. The temptation to deny, denigrate, or hide our gifts is real, as is the temptation to be arrogant or self-serving. Susan Nelson Dunfee warns about the sin of hiding, a tendency often found among women to deny and hide their contributions.[3] We should also be aware of the danger of taking credit for our God-given graces, gifts, and talents in order to affirm our own egos. Resisting the urge to do so helps us recognize the source and purpose of those gifts. How do we practice disciplines that empower us to receive, appreciate, use, and tend our gifts rather than to hide them or claim them as private possessions for private benefits?

One discipline is to *identify spiritual gifts*—the gifts of individual people or of a community, whether a local congregation, neighborhood, prayer group, or Sunday school class. These might include gifts named by Paul in Romans 12:6-8, 1 Corinthians 12:1-11, or Galatians 5:22-23; you might also identify other gifts. One way to practice this discipline is to speak or write the gifts in a list (without discussion or reflection), then go back to the list and meditate on it in silence. If the opportunity is available, reflect on the list with others and identify the strong gifts, the ones that are being called forth at this particular time, the ones that are crying out to be expressed and developed.

This exercise can actually be a healing experience. Many years ago when Maya Angelou was at a low ebb in her life, near suicide, she went to her friend Wilkie for consolation. He listened to her story and then insisted that she sit at the desk and write a list of things for which she was thankful. She resisted, but Wilkie insisted and she began to write, "I can hear. I can speak. I have a son. . . ." When she finished writing, she felt renewed. Wilkie asked her to write one more thing: "I am blessed. And I am grateful." She did, and she left, without needing further consolation from her friend.[4]

Another discipline is to *give thanks daily for blessings received*. Some time ago, a friend of mine was released from her ministry in a local church after many years of very strong service. She was devastated to learn this news, even more so because the notice was short and no reason was given. As a way of surviving, she began a discipline of writing five things in a gratitude journal every night— five things for which she was grateful during that particular day. In so doing, she was preparing for whatever new opportunities opened for her in this distressing situation.

Dietrich Bonhoeffer tells a similar story of an older, dying woman who was convinced that she had been cast away by God. Nothing could console her. Finally, on her last day of life a pastor asked if she had given thanks for her life. She was not sure, so he prayed with her at length and "uplifted her whole life in thanksgiving."[5] This prayer released her from whatever had been taunting her, and she died in peace. Bonhoeffer argues that spiritual trials emerge when we are unthankful before God. Then he adds two other causes of spiritual trial—hopelessness regarding what God can do (thinking it is too late) or holding on to unconfessed sin.[6] In short, he urges people to build honest and hopeful relationships with God and other people.

The two disciplines of identifying gifts and giving thanks to God are more than positive thinking. Being prepared is an act of hope—hope that God is with you now and that God's future will be real. With this in mind, we turn to the next theme.

Lighting the Way

The bridesmaids in Matthew's story were responsible for lighting the way for the bride and groom as they traveled. They had simple tools—lanterns and oil—and lighting the way involved using those tools to perform a designated function. In a deep sense, this simple tale points to a critical mission of the church: lighting the way into God's future using the simple tools that we are given to perform the functions to which we are called. To consider this challenge, we turn to a text in the Hebrew Bible (Old Testament) in which a simple, unnamed widow performed her functions with almost no tools at all. This is one of the stories that Jesus told that day when he stood to read the scroll in Nazareth before he was run out of town (Luke 4:25-26).

The widow of Zarephath is the woman who fed Elijah (1 Kings 17:8-16). In those days a drought covered the land—a drought that Elijah had called down in order to demonstrate Yahweh's power over King Ahab's Baal. In the days of this drought, Yahweh commanded the unnamed widow of Zarephath to feed Elijah. Then God sent Elijah to her. When Elijah reached the gate of Zarephath, he saw the widow gathering sticks. He said to her, "Bring me some water to drink." She went, but Elijah called out again, "Bring me some bread." She answered, "As the LORD your God lives, I do not have any food cooked, only a little meal and a little oil. I am gathering some sticks so that I can cook the meal and oil for myself and my son so that we may eat it and die." Elijah said, "Fear not. Go ahead and do what you said, but prepare me a small cake first. For Yahweh says, 'The jar of meal and the jug of oil will not be emptied until the day when the Lord sends rain.'" She did as Elijah said, and sure enough, she and he and her son ate for many days. The meal and the oil did not run out.

In this story, we find a woman preparing for death. But when she accepted an impossible task of baking bread with no ingredients, she began to prepare for life. Her gifts were meager, but she was prepared to use what she had. That was when something unbelievable happened: the meal and oil were mysteriously multiplied, just enough every day for her to prepare food for her family and guest to eat. As she did the impossible, going again and again to the empty jar and jug, the containers were not empty after all. For the widow of Zarephath to light the way was to take the circumstances that God presented, along with the meager gifts that she had, and to respond to God again and again. She simply used what she had to feed her son, her guest, and herself.

Not only does this story point to a miracle performed by an unnamed widow, but it also points to God's mission. Hence, Luke chooses to describe Jesus' telling of this same story right after proclaiming from the scroll, "The Spirit of the Lord is upon me" (Luke 4:17-18, 25-26). In this situation, Jesus has chosen not to perform glorious miracles but to remind his listeners of a miracle performed by the widow of Zarephath, a poor Gentile woman—a lowly person by almost any social standards of their day or hers. This message is easily missed, even by modern commentators on the widow's story in 1 Kings or Jesus' story in Luke. They often accentuate Elijah as the source of the miracle;[7] Jesus accentuated the Gentile widow.

What disciplines can guide Christians today in lighting the way? One is to *be aware of the way in which simple people, past and present, already light the way to see God's future.* Ask of everything you meet in God's world—every biblical text, story, hymn, neighbor, community, and natural wonder: How does this text or experience point to God's future? Another discipline is to *meditate and reflect on where the points of pain exist in your community and in the larger world:* What is required of you in order to respond to these points of pain? How might you light the way?

Welcoming and Offering Companionship

This discussion leads naturally to a third theme in the story of the bridesmaids—welcoming and offering companionship. The maidens had responsibility to welcome the bride and groom and travel with them to the groom's home. The story's double reference to an ordinary bridegroom and to Jesus fits a common pattern in early Christian literature to describe Jesus as a bridegroom. The double reference suggests the double importance of welcoming and walking with ordinary people and also with Jesus.

In fact, walking with ordinary people *is* walking with Jesus. This emphasis reappears in Matthew when he describes the judgment. At the time of judgment, the Son of Man will judge who is to inherit the kingdom. He will say to the righteous:

> I was hungry and you gave me food, I was thirsty and you gave me something to drink, I was a stranger and you welcomed me, I was naked and you gave me clothing, I was sick and you took care of me, I was in prison and you visited me.
>
> (Matthew 25:35-36)

When the people ask the Lord when they did these things, the Lord will reply, "Truly I tell you, just as you did it to one of the least of these who are members of my family, you did it to me" (25:40). We see here the echo of Matthew's story of the bridesmaids. Ministry to ordinary people (like a bride and groom, or the hungry and sick) corresponds with ministry to Jesus.

At least four disciplines can undergird the Christian mission of welcoming and offering companionship. First, *ask who needs to be welcomed in your community and in your life.* Whether you turn to a popular novel such as John Grisham's *The Street Lawyer* or a film such as *Patch Adams,* you find people pouring out this question in contemporary United States culture. People who are homeless, poor, ill, or cast out of the mainstream due to their race, creed, culture, or sexual orientation cry out to be welcomed. The cry is not for shallow attention but for deep companionship.

This need leads naturally to a second discipline, to *reflect with others on how genuine hospitality can be offered.* One of the reasons that the church is so torn apart by homosexuality is that points of view (opinions, perspectives, interpretations) have been allowed to take precedence over people. The church needs to continue dialogue on points of view; yet it could, at the same time, offer full welcome and companionship to all people. Hospitality is a theme deep in Jewish and Christian scriptures; thus, reflection on opportunities for genuine hospitality can draw deeply from our biblical heritage as well as from the hurts of our contemporary world.

Abraham and Sarah offered hospitality by entertaining three strangers, only later to realize that the Lord was in their company. Within this context of hospitality, the Lord told them they would have a child (Genesis 18:1-15). We see countless other references to hospitality throughout Scripture, including the familiar Psalm 23:5: "You prepare a table before me in the presence of my enemies." Ironically, one of the biblical texts that is often used to critique homosexuality (Genesis 19:1-28) speaks more directly to the violation of hospitality than to sexual orientation. This is reinforced in Ezekiel 16:49-50 and Matthew 10:14-15. Even recognizing varied interpretations of the text in relation to sexuality, the injunction to hospitality is crystal clear. Similarly, Matthew's charge to care for the sick and visit the imprisoned (25:31-46) continues the injunction to offer hospitality with all who have need. These are all texts for our continuing reflection.

This discussion leads naturally to a third discipline, namely to *engage in acts of hospitality with the people and parts of God's creation who are crying to be welcomed.* This sounds quite simple, but people are usually tempted to study issues and questions for many months or years before acting. A priest in Los Angeles asked local churches to buy old hotels on Skid Row before the buildings were bought by businesses and converted to other purposes. Some church leaders were fearful that buying such property without having money to renovate and begin a major housing program would simply make them "slum landlords." The priest responded, "Just take this first step before it is too late; then you can take the next step when you are able." In short, this priest was being very practical, but she was also crying out for urgent acts of hospitality.

The fourth discipline naturally follows this one: to *critique and transform your actions as you journey.* The priest of the Skid Row story was wise indeed; she knew that local churches, once they had purchased slum property, could not (or should not) hold on to that property without asking ethical questions about how to relate with the hotel residents. She hoped that their action to purchase these properties would lead to their ongoing critique and transformation of action. In the meantime, the urgent need to buy the hotels would be addressed. Critique and transformation need to be part of all acts of welcome and companionship. Even well-intentioned acts may lead to unexpected negative consequences. Further, the actions of one year may need to shift dramatically in the next.

This practice of critique and transformation is a powerful part of Wesleyan and other Christian traditions. In John Wesley's class meetings, people were encouraged to reflect on their daily lives and critique themselves within communities of accountability. Congregations are also invited to reflect honestly on their community life. In Wesley's classes and bands, people gathered each week to pray, read Scripture, and reflect on their lives, especially on their actions of the preceding week. Similar practices are part of "base communities" in Latin America.[8] The purpose of critique and transformation is to become more self-conscious and to grow in faith. Self-consciousness includes awareness of one's deepest commitments and experiences of God, and awareness of sin in oneself and the larger society. The assumption in the classes of Methodism and the base communities of Latin America is that self-examination is a pathway by which God acts, opening people to new tugs of God's Spirit. These classes and base communities have value for the participants, but also for the larger church and the larger community. Consider the spiritual renewal and the anti-slavery movements that emerged out of early Methodism.

The disciplines identified in this section involve reflecting, acting, and critiquing our ministries. The last discipline of critique accompanies ministries of hospitality because acts of hospitality lead naturally to new moments in a person's or community's life, thus beginning the circle of reflection and action again.

Celebrating

Finally, the story of the bridesmaids leads to celebration—a grand wedding banquet! As a "kingdom of heaven" story, so familiar in Matthew, this story has a happy ending, at least for a moment. The wise bridesmaids had enough oil for the long wait, and they were able to see the bridegroom coming, to welcome the bride and groom, and to travel with them to a great party in the home of the groom. In this story, Matthew compares the kingdom of heaven to a father's wedding feast for his son (reminiscent of the same metaphor in Matthew 22:2). Such wedding feasts were common practice in that time and place, usually following a ceremony in the bride's home.

The inherent missional challenge is to join in the celebration—receiving opportunities to celebrate, taking responsibilities that are yours, discerning urgent moments for celebration, and entering the feast joyfully. Note that the wedding feast in the bridesmaids' story was not created by the bridesmaids; they were invited, they followed, and they entered. This is true of many of the celebrations described in Matthew. Celebration is a gift, and people are simply expected to play their part. Perhaps our fretful efforts to create celebrations run counter to the joy of playing one's simple part and then simply entering the festivities. Certainly the celebration of this story invites people to share joy and a festive meal—a covenantal celebration!

Some aspects of this story distract from the celebration, however. First, the bride is implied but is not explicitly named, revealing something of the patriarchal culture. It also reveals Matthew's intention to highlight Jesus by drawing a correspondence between the bridegroom and Jesus. Another revealing aspect of the story is the long wait for the bridegroom's delayed arrival. Matthew seems to be preparing his listeners for a long, uncertain wait for Jesus' return. This story is a waiting story, which raises anxiety and makes the final celebration all the more welcome.

On the other hand, the most distracting element of this story is the late arrival of the unprepared bridesmaids. They went somewhere to get more lamp oil and returned to the banquet late. When they requested entrance, they were denied. This motif is familiar in Matthew. Matthew frequently emphasized that not everyone would enter the kingdom of heaven; some would be wise, and some foolish (7:21-27). He also emphasized the importance of keeping awake, "for you know neither the day nor the hour" (25:13; see also 24:42-44). These warnings are underscored in Matthew, where they are presented as Jesus' last teachings before the trial and crucifixion. They seem to be the teachings that Matthew wants people to remember as they reflect on Jesus' life and death.

Even with these hard messages, however, the story ends with celebration—a feast. The thrust of the story seems to be one of invitation and urgency. The hope is that everyone *will* be prepared and *will* enter the feast! The story is told not to discourage and destroy, but to encourage people to expect a feast and prepare for it. The warnings fit with Matthew's interest in the kingdom of heaven, but they might also be translated for other contexts where expecting and preparing are important. For example, some opportunities do not come again: a visit to someone who is dying in the hospital, a word of thank-you to someone you will not see again, an action to protect waters threatened by toxic dumping, a response to inflammatory or destructive racial actions in your community, or a word of assurance to someone who feels deserted by God. Although Jesus' story of the bridesmaids does not address such situations directly, the story does point to opportunities, responsibilities, and urgency. It is, thus, suggestive of disciplines.

The first discipline is to *seek opportunities to celebrate within your congregation, family, or larger community*. What celebrations already exist? What opportunities are available if people will simply stop and notice? A second discipline is to *take responsibility to invite others, to prepare, and to enjoy the celebrations*. Celebrations are not solely produced by human effort, but they require a lot of human energy—spreading invitations, preparing the details with care, and preparing ourselves to participate fully. In this sense, we are co-creators with God. A third discipline is to *discern and respond to moments of urgency*. Some celebrations are fleeting and will not come again. The practice of discernment can awaken people to fleeting opportunities as well as ordinary ones. In such moments of urgency, people might stop what they are doing to engage fully in the passing, festive moment. A fourth discipline is the most obvious and the most important—*enjoy*! Celebration, after all, is a time of joy. Participation is not for the sake of doing one's duty; it is a time of dancing with joy.

Come to the Covenant Table

The story of the maidens and their lamps leads to a great feast—a covenantal act. The discussion of calling and future has, thus, led back to the covenant—the theme with which this book began.

Covenant is a gathering at Table—to eat and enjoy, and to be bound again in covenant with God, our companions at the Table, and the whole of God's creation. The Table is both a gathering place and a celebrating place; it is also a place where people enter covenant with differences, irritations, fears, and hopes. The following poem was inspired by the promise of coming to the Table.

Come to the Table if you want to eat;
Come to the Table where all can meet;
Come to the Table if you want to share;
Come to the Table, but only if you dare.
Eating at the Table is a covenantal act;
When we meet at Table, we enter a pact;
We are invited and challenged to share our lives,
And we will be changed; narrowness dies!

Imagine the Table:
Some lay out tapa cloth; others want straight chairs;
Some eat simply; others spread gourmet fare;
Some drink wine; others drink juice;
Some want chitlins, and others want goose.
Some defer to women; others to men;
Some eat meat; others think that's a sin.

Imagine the Table:
Some drink from their bowls; for others, spoons are best.
Some eat with chopsticks; some eat with their hands,
    even with guests.
Some eat quietly, while others slurp.
Some say thank you, and some thank with a burp.

Gathering at the Table is no easy affair;
Perhaps that's why eating with strangers is rare.
But strangers are our neighbors
And love is our call
And Jesus ate with outcasts—one and all!

If we are to join in the future of God,
We will come to the Table and share of our best;
We will act so everyone eats well at the fest;
We will do all we can so justice can grow;
We will love all God's people and then we will know

That, however sick the world may be,
God's power and love can set people free!

By Mary Elizabeth Mullino Moore, March 1999.

This poem suggests some of the risk involved in a ministry of coming to the Table. People face *personal risks,* making themselves vulnerable to others, especially people who are different from themselves, whether in race, gender, culture, sexual orientation, or theological view. People also face *social risks*—inviting all people to the Table. Just as food and eating evoke deep emotions, so do food issues evoke controversy in local churches, especially when two or more congregations are sharing facilities or when great diversity exists within one congregation. The social risks that people face also have to do with vulnerability—the uncertainty, intimidation, and distrust that emerges when people come to the Table with all of their differences. People also face *religious risks* because gathering at a common Table is a covenantal act. Whether or not we like those who gather with us, we are bound by sharing in God's grace and our mutual commitment of friendship and hospitality at God's Table.

The challenge of coming to Table is at the heart of the teaching of Paul, who described the church as one body with many members (1 Corinthians 12:12-31) and described covenant in relation to Christian living (Galatians). Covenant has to do with oneness and diversity, with gathering and scattering, with living our full lives with love for God and neighbor. In the midst of a workshop on racism and hope, I realized that one could be playful with the image of Table as an acronym for Christian living. Consider the concrete proposals for action that emerge from T-A-B-L-E.

T—**Trust** in God, who created goodness, and trust in people, who are precious creations of God. Much violence is done in this world because people fear violence from others. Violence often emerges from distrust of others and of God. Trust is not naive; it is a constant searching for that which is strong and good, even in the midst of the most devastating evil.

A—Act on what you know. Most problems in the world are perpetuated not by a lack of knowledge but by a lack of will. What do we already know of God, and of hard and beautiful realities in our world? What do we know about ourselves? What kind of action is called forth at this moment? In the words of contributing author Lydia Waters, acting requires that we "hate sin and live holy." In the words of contributing author Lily Villamin, it requires that we take responsibility as "partners with God in creating the future." Different members of our writing team use these different words, but the sense of God's call to action is strong for us all.

B—Build on the good that already exists. Not only do we not need to reinvent the wheel, but we have much to learn from traditions, actions, and powerful communities of the past and present. The belief that we each need to create a new world that is completely different from what others have created is arrogant and destructively competitive.

L—Look into ourselves and our world. We need to engage in self-examination, critical reflection on our communities, and constant study of our world, whether through talking with others or reading newspapers and books. We need, also, to look and listen through meditation and contemplation, simply being still and allowing God to reveal the fullness and urgencies of the world.

E—Effect change. Christians are called to be and to do. To live faithfully is to pray that God will give us "serenity to accept what cannot be changed, courage to change what should be changed, and wisdom to distinguish the one from the other."[9] We are called to change our visions, change ourselves, change public policy, and change our way of doing church. Change requires opening ourselves to God so that we will want to be healed, so that our wills will be transformed, so that the work of our hands will be blessed. Change in itself is not always good, but with the power and guidance of God's Spirit, we might be changed in wondrous ways. In the Wesleyan tradition, John Wesley spoke of the possibility of perfection; in the biblical tradition, all things are possible. Neither of those images was put forth naively, but they are bold affirmations that God can work miracles in changing our lives and the lives of our congregations and communities.

These are the challenges of coming to the Table—entering the feast that is spread before us. They are also the challenges of living as covenant community, called to live with God and for God. Just as the Jewish meal at Table begins and ends with prayer, so none of these actions are possible outside of a grateful and honest relationship with God. The hope for genuine faithfulness rests finally in God, who provides, abides, and empowers. May it be so!

Conclusion

Resources for Meditation

Read and sing selected hymns from numbers 700–734 of *The United Methodist Hymnal*. These hymns are grouped under the title "New Heaven and a New Earth." Identify the different visions of God's future represented in these diverse hymns, and discuss the ones that seem most powerful for you. Choose one or two of these hymns for daily meditation over the next week. If you are studying this book with a group, sing selections chosen by the group, both before and after your days of personal meditation.

Questions for Reflection

- List and reflect upon each of the disciplines identified in the "Call to God's Future" section of this chapter. Disciplines are listed (and italicized) under each challenge named in that section: being prepared, lighting the way, welcoming and offering companionship, and celebrating. Reflect on the value of these disciplines, and choose one or two that you will practice in the coming week. Also, reflect on the disciplines that would be most valuable for your congregation or community. Consider ways in which your community might practice these disciplines.
- Consider the concluding challenge of coming to the Table. Where are the places in your life right now where you are called to trust,

act, build, look, and effect change? Where are these places in the life of your community?

Endnotes

1 See *Matthew: Evangelist and Teacher*, by R.T. France (The Paternoster Press, 1989); pages 276–278.

2 This accent on practice is strong in Matthew's Gospel. See elaboration in *Matthew: Evangelist and Teacher*, by R.T. France (The Paternoster Press, 1989); pages 260-278.

3 See *Beyond Servanthood: Christianity and the Liberation of Women*, by Susan Nelson Dunfee (University Press of America, 1989); especially pages 105–130. This author is now exploring the reality that women—especially women of color—sometimes use hiding as a way of survival; but the attention of this earlier book is directed to the use of hiding as an escape from full selfhood rather than as a chosen strategy to survive oppression.

4 See *Singin' and Swingin' and Gettin' Merry Like Christmas*, by Maya Angelou (Random House, 1976); pages 260–263.

5 From *Spiritual Care*, by Dietrich Bonhoeffer, translated by Jay C. Rochelle (Fortress Press, 1985); pages 53–54.

6 See *Spiritual Care*, by Dietrich Bonhoeffer, translated by Jay C. Rochelle (Fortress Press, 1985); pages 53–55.

7 The emphasis is placed on Elijah's words and acts in *Word Biblical Commentary, Volume 12, 1 Kings*, by Simon J. DeVries (Word Books, 1985); pages 216–217; *1 Kings With an Introduction to Historical Literature*, by Burke O. Long (William B. Eerdmans Publishing Company, 1984); pages 181–182; and *All of the Women of the Bible*, by Edith Deen (Harper & Brothers Publishers, 1955); page 134.

8 See *Ecclesiogenesis: The Base Communities Reinvent the Church*, by Leonardo Boff, translated by Robert R. Barr (Orbis Books, 1986).

9 As quoted in *Courage to Change: An Introduction to the Life and Thought of Reinhold Niebuhr*, by June Bingham (Charles Scribner's Sons, 1961); frontispage. There are several stories about the origin of this prayer. The most widely recognized is that Reinhold Niebuhr wrote it for a worship service in 1934 and gave it away to a neighbor who asked for it after the service. The neighbor, Dr. Howard Robbins, published it the following year as part of a pamphlet of prayers. It has been used widely by Alcoholics Anonymous, the U.S.O., the National Council of Churches, and other organizations.